Coast Guard

AUXILIARY BOAT CREW QUALIFICATION GUIDE, VOLUME II: COXSWAIN

COMDTINST M16794.53A
January 2007

U.S. Department of
Homeland Security

United States
Coast Guard

Commandant
United States Coast Guard

2100 Second St., S.W.
Washington, DC 20593-0001
Staff Symbol: CG-3PCX
Phone: (202) 372-1271

COMDTINST M16794.53A
05 JAN 2007

COMMANDANT INSTRUCTION M16794.53A

Subj: AUXILIARY BOAT CREW QUALIFICATION GUIDE, VOLUME II: COXSWAIN

Ref: (a) Auxiliary Manual, COMDTINST M16790.1 (series)
       (b) Boat Crew Seamanship Manual, COMDTINST M16114.5 (series)
       (c) Auxiliary Boat Crew Training Manual, COMDTINST M16794.51 (series)
       (d) Auxiliary Operations Policy Manual, COMDTINST M16798.3 (series)
       (e) Navigation Rules, International – Inland, COMDTINST M16672.2 (series)
       (f) U.S. Coast Guard Addendum to the United States National Search and
           Rescue Supplement (NSS) to the International Aeronautical and Maritime
           Search and Rescue Manual (IAMSAR), COMDTINST M16130.2 (series)

1. PURPOSE. This Manual establishes policies and procedures for the training,
   qualification, and certification of Auxiliary members for patrol duty on Coast Guard
   Auxiliary vessel facilities.

2. ACTION. Area, district, and sector commanders, commanders of maintenance and
   logistics commands, commanding officers of integrated support commands,
   commanding officers of headquarters units, assistant commandants for directorates,
   Judge Advocate General and special staff elements at Headquarters shall ensure
   compliance with the provisions of this Notice. Internet release is authorized.

3. DIRECTIVES AFFECTED.

   a. Effective 01 January 2007, the Auxiliary Boat Crew Qualification Guide, Volume
      II: Coxswain, COMDTINST M16794.53 is cancelled.

   b. Where the provisions of this Manual differ from the Auxiliary Manual,
      COMDTINST M16790.1 (series), the provisions of this Manual shall apply.

4. DISCUSSION. This Manual is part of the complete revision of the Coast Guard's

DISTRIBUTION – SDL No.146

	a	b	c	d	e	f	g	h	i	j	k	l	m	n	o	p	q	r	s	t	u	v	w	x	y	z
A																										
B		8	10		1																					
C									2		2			2									2		2	2
D																										
E									2	2	2							2	2							
F																										
G																										
H																										

NON STANDARD DISTRIBUTION: Auxiliary National Supply Center, NEXCOM, NADCO-CG/SS, DC-O, DCV-OS

~~family of boat crew training and qualification publications. These publications are~~ being revised to reflect the best and safest practices in the Coast Guard Auxiliary fleet.

5. <u>RESPONSIBILITY</u>. Commandant (CG-3PCX-2) is responsible for the content and upkeep of this Manual. Questions or concerns about the material contained in this Manual should be addressed to Commandant (CG-3PCX) at (202) 372-1271.

6. <u>ENVIRONMENTAL ASPECT AND IMPACT CONSIDERATIONS</u>. Environmental considerations were examined in the development of this Manual and have been determined to be not applicable.

7. <u>FORMS/REPORTS</u>. The Coast Guard (CG) forms called for in this Manual are available on the internet at http://www.uscg.mil/ccs/cit/cim/forms1/welcome.htm. Coast Guard Auxiliary forms can be found at http://forms.cgaux.org/forms.html.

/s/
CRAIG E. BONE
Rear Admiral, U. S. Coast Guard
Assistant Commandant for Prevention

RECORD OF CHANGES

CHANGE NUMBER	DATE OF CHANGE	DATE ENTERED	BY WHOM ENTERED

(This page intentionally left blank)

Table of Contents

Chapter 2   Coxswain Qualification Tasks - (Continued)

Chapter 2   Coxswain Qualification Tasks - (Continued)

(This page intentionally left blank)

Chapter 1.   Introduction

Overview

The Auxiliary Boat Crew Qualification Guides are an integral part of the boat crew qualification and certification process. Each volume contains a collection of tasks which must be learned, practiced, and performed by the trainee. These tasks represent the minimum elements of skill and knowledge necessary for safe and effective performance as a Coast Guard Auxiliary boat crew member. This chapter contains three sections:

- Section A: Purpose

- Section B: Description of the Guide

- Section C: The Qualification Process

Section A.   Purpose

A.1. The Qualification Guide

This Qualification Guide is used in conjunction with the Auxiliary Boat Crew Training Manual, COMDTINST M16794.51 (series), the Auxiliary Operations Policy Manual, COMDTINST M16798.3 (series) and the Boat Crew Seamanship Manual, COMDTINST M16114.5 (series), to train and qualify Auxiliary members to serve as crew members on Auxiliary vessel facilities.

This Qualification Guide contains a series of tasks that are performed by Auxiliary members to demonstrate that they possess the knowledge and skills required to serve as an Auxiliary coxswain. Upon successful completion of all tasks in the Qualification Guide, including the dockside oral exam and underway check ride with a Qualification Examiner, the member is qualified.

A.2. Training Goal

The goal of the training program is to enable people to learn and perform up to their full potential in Auxiliary surface operations missions. This qualification guide, together with the mentoring process, is designed to lead members through a training program at a learning pace suitable for each individual. The purpose of the boat crew training program is not to "weed out" or exclude people. Rather, it is to qualify and certify as many volunteers as possible, without compromising mission integrity and safety.

Section B.   Description of the Guide

B.1. Format

The Qualification Guide consists of three volumes:

- Volume I: Crew Member
- Volume II: Coxswain
- Volume III: Personal Watercraft (PWC) Operator

Each volume has two chapters:

- Chapter 1: Introduction
- Chapter 2: Qualification Tasks

B.2. Qualification Tasks

Each qualification task represents a certain skill or piece of knowledge required in the performance of duty as an Auxiliary boat crew member. Collectively, the complete set of tasks represents the minimum performance standard for the position. Each task has seven parts:

- Designation
- Title
- References
- Conditions
- Standards
- Performance Criteria
- Verification

B.2.a. Designation

Each task is designated by a number in the following format:

BCM-02-03-AUX

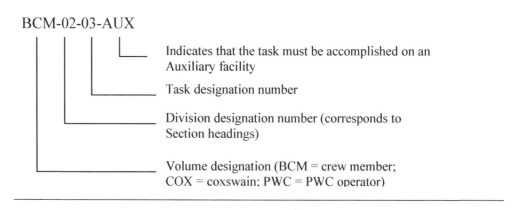

Indicates that the task must be accomplished on an Auxiliary facility

Task designation number

Division designation number (corresponds to Section headings)

Volume designation (BCM = crew member; COX = coxswain; PWC = PWC operator)

B.2.b. Title	The name and general nature of the task.

B.2.c. Reference	Lists sources of teaching material, background information, and policy. The primary reference for seamanship skills is reference (b). Other references shown in this guide are Coast Guard policy or technical directives. However, members are encouraged to use a wide range of references for small boat handling, navigation, and seamanship skills. Reference (c) has an extensive list of references, including the Auxiliary Specialty courses and the Auxiliary Public Education courses.

B.2.d. Conditions   Describes the environment and physical circumstances in which the task must be performed. Any tools or special equipment needed for completion of the task are listed here. The following terms are used in the Conditions and Standards sections of the tasks:

Boat Operations
Slow: Underway and moving ahead at clutch speed or slower.
Underway: Not tied to a pier or float and not anchored or moored.

Visibility
Restricted: Visibility less than ¼ mile.
Clear: All other states of visibility.

Sea Conditions
Calm: Waves less than 1 foot.
Moderate: Waves 1 to 4 feet.
Heavy: Waves 4 feet and over.

B.2.e. Standards   Standards describe the expected outcome of the task. Successful task completion is a function of how well a student is able to complete the task without assistance. Generally the task performance standards are as follows.

- **Knowledge Tasks:** Candidate must be able to cite, from memory, the required information. Mentors may wish to ask questions concerning particular steps for accomplishment in order to measure the candidate's total comprehension of the subject matter.

- **Skill Tasks:** Candidate must be able to personally perform all performance tasks without prompting or assistance from the mentor. Each task demonstration must follow the correct sequence with little or no hesitation between the steps for accomplishment.

B.2.f. Performance Criteria — These steps delineate the procedure that is best followed for performing each task. They can be utilized two basic ways.

- **To Aid in Learning the Task:** Some steps for task accomplishment follow exact procedures which are required for performing a particular operation or using a specific piece of equipment, while others serve as general guidelines for task completion.

- **To Provide a Performance Check:** The steps provide a check list which can be used by the mentor to evaluate the trainee's performance.

B.2.g. Verification — The designated mentor must print his/her name, sign and date this line attesting that the candidate successfully performed the task in accordance with the prescribed standards. The mentor does not need to initial or sign each performance criterion.

B.3. Additional Standards — No additional qualification tasks or modification of task therein may be required to achieve either qualification or certification. The tasks (not including waiverable tasks) in each volume of the Qualification Guide represent a uniform, national standard for qualification and certification. National standard tasks may be altered with CHDIRAUX approval. A member who successfully completes the national standard tasks is entitled to be certified by the Director, and to earn appropriate recognition, including certificates, insignia, and ribbons.

Order-issuing authorities may require additional training, based on local operational considerations, prior to assigning a certified member to boat crew duty.

B.4. Waiverable Tasks — Certain tasks in the Qualification Guides are designated as "**Waiverable Tasks by DIRAUX**". The Director may waive these designated tasks on a case-by-case basis given the mission requirements, the nature of the waters, or if the task is not operationally required for the geographical area.

Section C.   The Qualification Process

C.1. Process Summary	For a complete description of the training and qualification process and policies, refer to reference (c). The process is summarized below.

A series of **qualification tasks** defines the knowledge and skills required for each boat crew position. Each task describes a certain job skill, and states performance criteria for that skill. For example, a qualification task for the coxswain position is to take a vessel in stern tow. The trainee completes the task by reading the reference material listed, reviewing the skills with a mentor, and then practicing the task. When the trainee demonstrates mastery of the task, the mentor signs off the task. When a mentor signs off all tasks for a certain position, the trainee is then scheduled for a check ride for certification with a **Qualification Examiner, or (QE)** in accordance with reference (c). The QE is an experienced Auxiliary coxswain appointed by the Director of Auxiliary to verify the proper completion of tasks. When the QE signs off the trainee's **Dockside Oral Exam** and **Underway Check Ride** tasks and is satisfied with the trainee's ability, the QE submits a recommendation to the Director, who then **certifies** the member. The member **maintains currency** of certification by meeting the standards outlined in reference (c).

C.2. Sign-Off Process	The process for learning and signing-off tasks is summarized below:

1. The mentor and trainee develop a work plan. This includes how many tasks will be assigned, whether tasks will be learned individually or in groups, scheduling on-the-water sessions, etc.

2. For each task, the mentor and trainee gather necessary reference material for the trainee to study. The trainee should complete the applicable sections of Chapter Three (Study Guide) that apply to the assigned tasks. Through a combination of self-study of written material and hands-on practice, the trainee learns skills required for the task.

3. The mentor demonstrates the task using procedures outlined in the qualification guide.

4. The mentor walks the trainee through the task until satisfied that the basic principles are understood.

5. The trainee practices the task until the mentor is confident that the trainee is able to consistently meet the task standards on his/her own.

C.2.	**Sign-Off Process (Continued)**	6. When satisfied that the trainee meets the standard, the mentor verifies completion by signing off the task at the bottom of the task page.
C.3.	**Qualification Examination**	The final step in the qualification process is examination by a Qualification Examiner (QE). Under the QE's direction, the trainee will complete a dockside oral examination and an underway check ride. Upon successful completion of these task, the member is now qualified. The details of this process are described in Chapter 3 of reference (c). Once qualified, the member is then certified by the Director. See Chapter 4 of reference (c) for a complete description of the certification process.

Appendix A – Training Plan

Training Plan - Inport Tasks

Task Number	Task name	Required Materials
COX-01-02-AUX	Complete The Incident Command System (ICS) Courses	On-line Curriculum and Exam or Correspondence Courses
COX-02-01-AUX	Describe The Indicators Of Approaching Heavy Weather	
COX-02-02-AUX	Recognize Warning Signs Of An Unstable Vessel	
COX-02-03-AUX	State The Procedures To Follow If Engine Will Not Start	
COX-02-04-AUX	State The Procedures To Follow For Loss Of Electrical Power	
COX-02-05-AUX	State The Procedures To Follow For High Engine Temperature	
COX-02-06-AUX	State Procedures To Follow For Low/No Engine Oil Pressure	
COX-02-07-AUX	State The Procedures To Follow For Defective Charging System	
COX-02-08-AUX	State The Procedures To Follow For Shaft Vibration	
COX-02-09-AUX	State The Procedures To Follow For A Steering Casualty	
COX-03-01-AUX	State The Forces That Affect Boat Handling	
COX-03-02-AUX	State The Basic Principles Of Boat Handling	
COX-03-03-AUX	State The Operational Limitations And Characteristics Of The Facility	
COX-04-01-AUX	Successfully Complete The Navigation Rules Of The Road Exam	
COX-05-01-AUX	Identify Navigational Publications	Coast Pilot, Light List, Local Notice To Mariners, Tide Tables, Tidal Current Tables, Navigation Rules Inland-International COMDTINST M16672.2 (series)
COX-05-03-AUX	Determine A Compass Course From True Course	Chart, Aux Facility Deviation Table, Plotting Tools
COX-05-04-AUX	Sketch A Chart Of The Local Operating Area	Pencil, Paper
COX-06-01-AUX	Organization And Responsibility	
COX-06-02-AUX	Legal Aspects And USCG Policies	
COX-06-03-AUX	SAR Emergency Phases	
COX-06-04-AUX	State The Basic Concepts Related To Search Planning	

Training Plan - Inport Tasks (continued)

Task Number	Task name	Required Materials
COX-06-05-AUX	Plot A Single Unit Expanding Square Search Pattern (SS)	Charts, Search Action Plan
COX-06-06-AUX	Plot A Single Unit Sector Search Pattern (VS)	Charts, Search Action Plan
COX-06-07-AUX	Plot A Single Unit Parallel Search Pattern (PS)	Charts, Search Action Plan
COX-06-08-AUX	Plot A Single Unit Trackline Return Search Pattern (TSR)	Charts, Search Action Plan
COX-06-10-AUX	Obtain Distress Information And Pass To The Controlling Shore Unit	
COX-07-04-AUX	State The Action To Take If Your Boat Was Aground	
COX-08-01-AUX	State General Towing Safety Procedures	
COX-08-02-AUX	State The Principle Forces That Effect Small Boat Towing	
COX-08-03-AUX	Inspect The Towline And Associated Hardware	
COX-09-01-AUX	Discuss Auxiliary Patrol Commander's Duties	
COX-09-02-AUX	Complete Administrative Tasks (Reports, Orders, Etc.)	CGAUX-26, CG-4612, CG-5132
COX-09-03-AUX	Complete the Operations Policy Manual and National SAR Plan Open Book Exam	QE, Exam
COX-09-05-AUX	Dockside Oral And Written Examination	QE

Training Plan - Underway Tasks

Task Number	Task name	Required Materials
All Tasks Require a properly Equipped Auxiliary Facility		
COX-01-01-AUX	Perform Twenty-Eight Hours Underway As Crew Member	
COX-03-04-AUX	Complete A Pre-Underway Check-Off For The Facility	Check Sheet, diagram
COX-03-05-AUX	Get The Boat Away From The Dock	
COX-03-06-AUX	Operate The Boat And Apply Its Handling Characteristics In Following, Head And Beam Seas	
COX-03-07-AUX	Maneuver A Boat In A Narrow Channel Or A River **(Waiverable By DIRAUX)**	
COX-03-08-AUX	Maneuver The Boat Alongside Another Boat With No Way On	
COX-03-09-AUX	Moor The Boat To A Dock	
COX-03-10-AUX	Anchor The Boat	
COX-03-11-AUX	Weigh The Boat's Anchor	
COX-04-02-AUX	Execute Commonly Used Sound Signals	
COX-04-03-AUX	Set The Proper Navigation Lights For Common Operational Boat Evolutions	
COX-05-02-AUX	Obtain A Visual Fix	Local Chart, Deviation Table, Hand Bearing Compass, Navigational Compass, Pencil, Parallel Ruler or Plotter
COX-05-05-AUX	Pilot A Boat Using Dead Reckoning Techniques	Compass, Speed/Engine RPM Curve or Speedometer, Stopwatch, Plotting Tools, Local Chart
COX-05-06-AUX	Pilot A Boat Using "Seaman's Eye"	Local Chart, Plotting tools
COX-05-07-AUX	Determine The Position Of A Boat Using Radar Ranges And Bearing **(If Equipped)**	Radar, Large Scale Chart, Navigation Kit, Fathometer
COX-05-08-AUX	Determine The Position Of A Boat Using GPS/DGPS **(If Equipped)**	Charts, Navigation Kit, D/GPS Receiver
COX-05-09-AUX	Determine The Position Of A Boat Using LORAN C **(If Equipped)**	Charts, Navigation Kit, LORAN C
COX-05-10-AUX	Determine Course To Steer And Speed Over Ground (SOG) Allowing For Set And Drift	Charts, Navigation Kit,

Training Plan - Underway Tasks (continued)

All Tasks Require a properly Equipped Auxiliary Facility

Task Number	Task name	Required Materials
COX-05-11-AUX	River Sailing, (Locks, Dams And Flood Warnings) And Pass Through A Lock **(Waiverable By DIRAUX)**	
COX-06-09-AUX	Execute A Search Pattern	Search Action Plan
COX-07-01-AUX	Determine The Approach To An Object And Station Keep	
COX-07-02-AUX	Recover A Person From The Water Using The Direct Pick Up Method	Oscar or substitute
COX-07-03-AUX	Approach A Burning Boat And Recover Personnel	Second Auxiliary Facility
COX-08-04-AUX	Make Preparations For Taking A Vessel In Tow	Second Auxiliary Facility
COX-08-05-AUX	Take A Vessel In Stern Tow	Second Auxiliary Facility
COX-08-06-AUX	Use A Shackle Or Kicker/Skiff Hook Assembly Connection To Take A Vessel In Stern Tow	Second Auxiliary Facility
COX-08-07-AUX	Take A Boat In Alongside Tow	Second Auxiliary Facility
COX-08-08-AUX	Moor A Disabled Vessel In Tow To A Float Or Pier	Second Auxiliary Facility
COX-09-04-AUX	Perform A Night Navigation And Piloting Exercise **(Waiverable By DIRAUX)**	
COX-09-06-AUX	Underway Check Ride	Second Auxiliary Facility, QE

Appendix B – Mentor Tracking Form

Trainee's Name: _____ **Member Number:** _____

Mentor/QE's Name (Printed)	Mentor/QE's Signature	Initials	Date

Section A Crew Efficiency Factors, Risk Factors and Team Coordination			
Task	**Description**	**QE Initials**	**Date**
COX-01-01-AUX	Perform Twenty-Eight Hours Underway As Crew Member		
COX-01-02-AUX	Complete The Incident Command System (ICS) Courses		

Section B Boat Characteristics, Stability, and Engineering			
Task	**Description**	**Mentor Initials**	**Date**
COX-02-01-AUX	Describe The Indicators Of Approaching Heavy Weather		
COX-02-02-AUX	Recognize Warning Signs Of An Unstable Vessel		
COX-02-03-AUX	State The Procedures To Follow If Engine Will Not Start		
COX-02-04-AUX	State The Procedures To Follow For Loss Of Electrical Power		
COX-02-05-AUX	State The Procedures To Follow For High Engine Temperature		
COX-02-06-AUX	State The Procedures To Follow For Low/No Engine Oil Pressure		
COX-02-07-AUX	State The Procedures To Follow For Defective Charging System		
COX-02-08-AUX	State The Procedures To Follow For Shaft Vibration		
COX-02-09-AUX	State The Procedures To Follow For A Steering Casualty		

	Section C Boat Handling		
Task	Description	Mentor Initials	Date
COX-03-01-AUX	State The Forces That Affect Boat Handling		
COX-03-02-AUX	State The Basic Principles Of Boat Handling		
COX-03-03-AUX	State The Operational Limitations And Characteristics Of The Facility		
COX-03-04-AUX	Complete A Pre-Underway Check Off For The Facility		
COX-03-05-AUX	Get The Boat Away From The Dock		
COX-03-06-AUX	Operate The Boat And Apply Its Handling Characteristics In Following, Head And Beam Seas		
COX-03-07-AUX	Maneuver A Boat In A Narrow Channel Or A River **(Waiverable By DIRAUX)**		
COX-03-08-AUX	Maneuver The Boat Alongside Another Boat With No Way On		
COX-03-09-AUX	Moor The Boat To A Dock		
COX-03-10-AUX	Anchor The Boat		
COX-03-11-AUX	Weigh The Boat's Anchor		

	Section D Rules of the Road		
Task	Description	Mentor/QE Initials	Date
COX-04-01-AUX	Successfully Complete The Navigation Rules Of The Road Exam		
COX-04-02-AUX	Execute Commonly Used Sound Signals		
COX-04-03-AUX	Set The Proper Navigation Lights For Common Operational Boat Evolutions		

	Section E *Piloting and Navigation*		
Task	**Description**	**Mentor Initials**	**Date**
COX-05-01-AUX	Identify Navigational Publications		
COX-05-02-AUX	Obtain A Visual Fix		
COX-05-03-AUX	Determine A Compass Course From True Course		
COX-05-04-AUX	Sketch A Chart Of The Local Operating Area		
COX-05-05-AUX	Pilot The Boat Using Dead Reckoning Techniques		
COX-05-06-AUX	Pilot A Boat Using "Seaman's Eye"		
COX-05-07-AUX	Determine The Position Of A Boat Using Radar Ranges And Bearing **(If Equipped)**		
COX-05-08-AUX	Determine The Position Of A Boat Using GPS/DGPS **(If Equipped)**		
COX-05-09-AUX	Determine The Position Of A Boat Using LORAN C **(If Equipped)**		
COX-05-10-AUX	Determine Course To Steer And Speed Over Ground (SOG), Allowing For Set And Drift		
COX-05-11-AUX	River Sailing, (Locks, Dams And Flood Warnings), And Pass Through A Lock **(Waiverable By DIRAUX)**		

Section F Search and Rescue			
Task	**Description**	**Mentor Initials**	**Date**
COX-06-01-AUX	Organization And Responsibility		
COX-06-02-AUX	Legal Aspects And USCG Policies		
COX-06-03-AUX	SAR Emergency Phases		
COX-06-04-AUX	State The Basic Concepts Related To Search Planning		
COX-06-05-AUX	Plot A Single Unit Expanding Square Search Pattern (SS)		
COX-06-06-AUX	Plot A Single Unit Sector Search Pattern (VS)		
COX-06-07-AUX	Plot A Single Unit Parallel Search Pattern(PS)		
COX-06-08-AUX	Plot A Single Trackline Return Search Pattern (TSR)		
COX-06-09-AUX	Execute A Search Pattern		
COX-06-10-AUX	Obtain Distress Information And Pass To The Controlling Shore Unit		

Section G Rescue and Assistance			
Task	**Description**	**Mentor Initials**	**Date**
COX-07-01-AUX	Determine The Approach And Station Keep		
COX-07-02-AUX	Recover A Person From The Water Using The Direct Pick Up Method		
COX-07-03-AUX	Approach A Burning Boat And Recover Personnel		
COX-07-04-AUX	State The Action To Take If Your Boat Was Aground		

Section H
Towing and Salvage

Task	Description	Mentor Initials	Date
COX-08-01-AUX	State General Towing Safety Precautions		
COX-08-02-AUX	State The Principle Forces That Effect Small Boat Towing		
COX-08-03-AUX	Inspect A Towline And Associated Hardware		
COX-08-04-AUX	Make Preparations For Taking A Vessel In Tow		
COX-08-05-AUX	Take A Vessel In Stern Tow		
COX-08-06-AUX	Use A Shackle Or Kicker/Skiff Hook Assembly Connection To Take A Vessel In Stern Tow		
COX-08-07-AUX	Take A Boat In Alongside Tow		
COX-08-08-AUX	Moor A Disabled Vessel In Tow To A Float Or Pier		

Section I
Auxiliary Specific Tasks

Task	Description	Mentor/QE Initials	Date
COX-09-01-AUX	Discuss Auxiliary Patrol Commander's Duties **(Waiverable By DIRAUX)**		
COX-09-02-AUX	Complete Administrative Tasks (Reports, Orders, Etc.)		
COX-09-03-AUX	Successfully Complete The Operations Policy Manual And National SAR Plan Open Book Exam		
COX-09-04-AUX	Perform A Night Navigation And Piloting Exercise **(Waiverable by DIRAUX)**		
COX-09-05-AUX	Dockside Oral Examination		
COX-09-06-AUX	Underway Check Ride		

Chapter 2   Coxswain Qualification Tasks

Overview

In this chapter

This chapter contains nine sections:

Section A.   Crew Efficiency Factors, Risk Factors And Team Coordination

Introduction

The following are the objectives of Section A:

- **Demonstrate** ability to perform duties as a certified Auxiliary Crew Member

In this section

This section contains two tasks:

Reading Assignment	Task Number	Task	See Page
None	COX-01-01-AUX	Perform Twenty-Eight Hours Underway As Crew Member	2-3
Course Curriculum	COX-01-02-AUX	Complete The Incident Command System (ICS) Courses	2-4

Name: _____

Task COX-01-01-AUX

Task	**Perform Twenty-Eight Hours Underway As Crew Member**
References	Auxiliary Operations Policy Manual, COMDTINST M16798.3 (series)
	Auxiliary Boat Crew Training Manual, COMDTINST M16794.51 (series)
Conditions	Performed while underway as a certified crew member on ordered patrols on an Auxiliary facility or Coast Guard boat.
Standards	Certified crew members must show proof of completing at least 28 hours underway on patrols.

Completed	**Performance Criteria**
_____	1. Member completed 28 hours underway on ordered patrols as certified Auxiliary or Coast Guard boat crew member.

Accomplished   **QE signature**_____   **Date**_____

Name: _____

Task COX-01-02-AUX

Task	**Complete The Incident Command System (ICS) Courses**
References	Federal Emergency Management Agency (FEMA) on-line courses or Coast Guard Correspondence courses.
Conditions	Task is conducted on-line or through Correspondence Courses.
Standards	The Trainee must show proof of completion.

Completed	**Performance Criteria**
_____	1. Passed the IS-100 Course.
_____	2. Passed the IS-200 Course.
_____	3. Passed the IS-700 Course.
_____	4. Passed the IS-800 Course.

Accomplished   **Mentor signature**_____   **Date**_____

Section B.   Boat Characteristics, Stability And Engineering

Introduction   The following are objectives of Section B:

- **Identify** and **Describe** the indicators of approaching weather.
- **Recognize** the signs of an unstable vessel.
- **Recognize** and **Perform** casualty control for various casualties.

In this section   This section contains nine tasks:

Reading Assignments	Task Number	Task	See Page
Ref (b) Chapter 12, Section A	COX-02-01-AUX	Describe The Indicators Of Approaching Heavy Weather	2-6
Ref (b) Chapter 9, All	COX-02-02-AUX	Recognize Warning Signs Of An Unstable Vessel	2-7
Ref (b) Chapter 8, Section E	COX-02-03-AUX	State The Procedures To Follow If Engine Will Not Start	2-8
Ref (b) Chapter 8, Section E	COX-02-04-AUX	State The Procedures To Follow For Loss Of Electrical Power	2-9
Ref (b) Chapter 8, Section E	COX-02-05-AUX	State The Procedures To Follow For High Engine Temperature	2-10
Ref (b) Chapter 8, Section E	COX-02-06-AUX	State The Procedures To Follow For Low/No Engine Oil Pressure	2-11
Ref (b) Chapter 8, Section E	COX-02-07-AUX	State The Procedures To Follow For Defective Charging System	2-12
Ref (b) Chapter 8, Section E	COX-02-08-AUX	State The Procedures To Follow For Shaft Vibration	2-13
Ref (b) Chapter 8, Section E	COX-02-09-AUX	State The Procedures To Follow For A Steering Casualty	2-14

Name: _____

Task COX-02-01-AUX

Task	**Describe The Indicators Of Approaching Heavy Weather**
References	Boat Crew Seamanship Manual, COMDTINST M16114.5 (series), Chapter 12
Conditions	Performed at any time ashore, at the dock, or afloat. Trainee must accomplish task without prompting or use of a reference.
Standards	In response to the mentor, the trainee must describe the indicators of approaching heavy weather.

Completed   **Performance Criteria**

_____   1. Listed six of the fifteen indicators of deteriorating weather.

_____   2. Listed four of the ten indicators of impending precipitation.

_____   3. Listed three of the seven indicators of impending strong winds.

Accomplished   **Mentor signature**_____ **Date**_____

Name: _____

Task COX-02-02-AUX

Task	**Recognize Warning Signs Of An Unstable Vessel**
References	Boat Crew Seamanship Manual, COMDTINST M16114.5 (series), Chapter 9
Conditions	Task should be performed underway observing other vessels in varying wind and sea conditions and when loaded differently (fishing vessels rigged/not rigged).
Standards	The visual observation must note: listing, set high or low in the water, trimmed by bow or stern, and wind/sea conditions. Compare your boat's reaction to sea conditions with the other boat(s).

Completed   **Performance Criteria**

_____   1. Determined if other vessel is listing.

_____   2. Determined if other vessel is riding high or low in the water.

_____   3. Determined if down by the bow, the stern, or even.

_____   4. Determined wind and sea conditions.

_____   5. Stated the causes and effects of the following:

        a.   free surface effect

        b.   downflooding

        c.   topside icing

        d.   free communication with the sea

Accomplished   **Mentor signature**_____   **Date**_____

Name: _____

Task COX-02-03-AUX

Task	**State The Procedures To Follow If Engine Will Not Start**
References	Boat Crew Seamanship Manual, COMDTINST M16114.5 (series), Chapter 8
Conditions	Performed at any time ashore, at the dock, or afloat. Trainee must accomplish task without prompting or use of a reference.
Standards	In response to the mentor, the trainee must describe or perform the procedures to follow if engine will not start.

Completed	**Performance Criteria**
_____	1. Anchor made ready.
_____	2. Informed controlling authority of situation and location, and stated the importance of keeping the controlling authority updated.
_____	3. Described the causes if engine fails to turn over.
_____	4. Stated corrective action to take when the engine fails to turn over.
_____	5. Described the causes if engine turns over but fails to start.
_____	6. State the corrective action to take if the engine turns over but fails to start.

Accomplished Mentor signature_____ Date_____

Name: _____

Task COX-02-04-AUX

Task	**State The Procedures To Follow For Loss Of Electrical Power**
References	Boat Crew Seamanship Manual, COMDTINST M16114.5 (series), Chapter 8
Conditions	Performed at any time ashore, at the dock, or afloat. Trainee must accomplish task without prompting or use of a reference.
Standards	In response to the mentor, the trainee must describe or perform the procedures to follow for loss of electrical power.

Completed   **Performance Criteria**

_____   1. Anchor made ready.

_____   2. Informed controlling authority of situation and location, and stated the importance of keeping the controlling authority updated on situation.

_____   3. Described the causes for loss of electrical power.

_____   4. State the corrective action to take for a loss of electrical power.

Accomplished   **Mentor signature**_____ **Date**_____

Name: _____

Task COX-02-05-AUX

Task	**State The Procedures To Follow For High Engine Temperature**
References	Boat Crew Seamanship Manual, COMDTINST M16114.5 (series), Chapter 8
Conditions	Performed at any time ashore, at the dock, or afloat. Trainee must accomplish task without prompting or use of a reference.
Standards	In response to the mentor, the trainee must describe or perform the procedures to follow for high engine temperature.

Completed   **Performance Criteria**

_____   1. Anchor made ready if underway.

_____   2. Informed controlling authority of situation and location, and stated the importance of keeping the controlling authority updated.

_____   3. Described the causes of high engine temperature.

_____   4. Stated the corrective action to take for high engine temperature.

_____   5. Stated procedure to follow when securing a hot engine.

Accomplished   Mentor signature_____   Date_____

Name: _____

Task COX-02-06-AUX

Task	**State The Procedures To Follow For Low/No Engine Oil Pressure**
References	Boat Crew Seamanship Manual, COMDTINST M16114.5 (series), Chapter 8
Conditions	Performed at any time ashore, at the dock, or afloat. Trainee must accomplish task without prompting or use of a reference.
Standards	In response to the mentor, the trainee must describe or perform the procedures to follow for low/no engine oil pressure.

Completed   **Performance Criteria**

_____   1. Anchor made ready.

_____   2. Informed controlling authority of situation and location, and stated the importance of keeping the controlling authority updated.

_____   3. Described the causes for low or no engine oil pressure.

_____   4. Stated the corrective action to take for low or no oil pressure.

Accomplished   **Mentor signature**_____   **Date**_____

Name: _____

Task COX-02-07-AUX

Task	**State The Procedures To Follow For Defective Charging System**
References	Boat Crew Seamanship Manual, COMDTINST M16114.5 (series), Chapter 8
Conditions	Performed at any time ashore, at the dock, or afloat. Trainee must accomplish task without prompting or use of a reference.
Standards	In response to the mentor, the trainee must describe or perform the procedures to follow for defective charging system.

Completed	Performance Criteria
_____	1. Anchor made ready if underway.
_____	2. Informed controlling authority of situation and location, and stated the importance of keeping the controlling authority updated.
_____	3. Described the causes of a defective charging system.
_____	4. State the corrective action to take for a defective charging system.

Accomplished   **Mentor signature**_____   **Date**_____

Name: _____

Task COX-02-08-AUX

Task	**State The Procedures To Follow For Shaft Vibration**
References	Boat Crew Seamanship Manual, COMDTINST M16114.5 (series), Chapter 8
Conditions	Performed at any time ashore, at the dock, or afloat. Trainee must accomplish task without prompting or use of a reference.
Standards	In response to the mentor, the trainee must describe or perform the procedures to follow for shaft vibration.

Completed   **Performance Criteria**

_____   1. Anchor made ready.

_____   2. Informed controlling authority of situation and location. Stated importance of keeping the controlling authority updated.

_____   3. Described the causes of a shaft vibration.

_____   4. Stated the corrective action to take for shaft vibration.

Accomplished   Mentor signature_____   Date_____

Name: _____

Task COX-02-09-AUX

Task	**State The Procedures To Follow For A Steering Casualty**
References	Boat Crew Seamanship Manual, COMDTINST M16114.5 (series), Chapter 8
Conditions	Performed at any time ashore, at the dock, or afloat. Trainee must accomplish task without prompting or use of a reference.
Standards	In response to the mentor, the trainee must describe or perform the procedures to follow for a steering casualty.

Completed   **Performance Criteria**

_____   1. Anchor made ready.

_____   2. Informed controlling authority of situation and location, and stated the importance of keeping the controlling authority updated.

_____   3. Described the causes of a steering casualty.

_____   4. Stated the corrective action to take for a steering casualty.

Accomplished   **Mentor signature**_____   **Date**_____

Section C.   Boat Handling

Introduction

The following are objectives for Section C:

- **Define** and **state** the principal forces that affect boat handling.

- **Handle** a boat proficiently during various common maneuvers.

- **State** the different safety aspects involved in boat handling.

In this section

This section contains eleven tasks:

Reading Assignments	Task Number	Task	See Page
Ref (b) Chapter 9, Section A Ref (b) Chapter 10, Section D	COX-03-01-AUX	State The Forces That Affect Boat Handling	2-16
Ref (b) Chapter 10, Section B	COX-03-02-AUX	State The Basic Principles Of Boat Handling	2-17
Ref (b) Chapter 2, Section A Ref (b) Chapter 8, Section B Ref (d) Chapter 1, Section I and J	COX-03-03-AUX	State The Operational Limitations And Characteristics Of The Facility	2-18
None	COX-03-04-AUX	Complete A Pre-Underway Check Off For The Facility	2-20
Ref (b) Chapter 10, Section D	COX-03-05-AUX	Get The Boat Away From The Dock	2-24
Ref (b) Chapter 10, Section F	COX-03-06-AUX	Operate The Boat And Apply Its Handling Characteristics In Following, Head And Beam Seas	2-25
Ref (b) Chapter 10, Sections F-G	COX-03-07-AUX	Maneuver A Boat In A Narrow Channel Or A River **(Waiverable By DIRAUX)**	2-27
Ref (b) Chapter 10, Section E	COX-03-08-AUX	Maneuver The Boat Alongside Another Boat With No Way On	2-29
Ref (b) Chapter 10, Section D	COX-03-09-AUX	Moor The Boat To A Dock	2-30
Ref (b) Chapter 10, Section H	COX-03-10-AUX	Anchor The Boat	2-31
Ref (b) Chapter 10, Section H	COX-03-11-AUX	Weigh The Boat's Anchor	2-33

Name: _____

Task COX-03-01-AUX

Task	**State The Forces That Affect Boat Handling**
References	Boat Crew Seamanship Manual, COMDTINST M16114.5 (series), Chapter 9 and 10
Conditions	Performed at any time ashore, at the dock or afloat. Trainee must accomplish task without prompting or use of a reference.
Standards	In response to the mentor, the trainee must state the forces that affect boat handling as outlined in the steps below.

Completed   **Performance Criteria**

_____ 1. Stated how weight and buoyancy affect a vessel's stability.

_____ 2. Stated how any change in the center of gravity of a boat affects stability when weight is added, subtracted, or shifted.

_____ 3. Stated how static force affects stability.

_____ 4. Stated how dynamic force affects stability.

_____ 5. Stated what affects the environmental forces of wind, seas, and current have on the horizontal motion of a vessel.

_____ 6. Stated the effect of running with a current.

_____ 7. Stated the effect of running against a current.

_____ 8. Stated the effect of leeway on a boat.

_____ 9. Stated how the cavitation of a boat's propeller affects boat handling.

_____ 10. Stated the effects of dynamic propeller thrust.

_____ 11. Stated the effects of "unequal blade thrust."

Accomplished   **Mentor signature**_____   **Date**_____

Name: _____

Task COX-03-02-AUX

Task	**State The Basic Principles Of Boat Handling**
References	Boat Crew Seamanship Manual, COMDTINST M16114.5 (series), Chapter 10
Conditions	Performed at any time ashore, at the dock, or afloat. Trainee must accomplish task without prompting or use of a reference.
Standards	In response to the mentor, the trainee must state the basic principles of boat handling listed in the steps below.

Completed   **Performance Criteria**

_____ 1. Stated the reaction of the boat with sternway on and the rudder amidships.

_____ 2. Stated the reaction of the boat with sternway on and the rudder left.

_____ 3. Stated the reaction of the boat with headway on and the rudder left.

_____ 4. Stated the reaction of the boat with headway on and the rudder right.

_____ 5. Stated the reaction of the boat when commencing forward motion from no way on.

_____ 6. Stated the reaction of a twin screw boat, when the port screw is placed ahead and the starboard screw in reverse.

_____ 7. Stated the reaction of a twin screw boat, with the port screw ahead and the starboard screw in reverse and turning the wheel to starboard.

_____ 8. Stated the reaction of a twin screw boat, with the port screw ahead and the starboard screw in reverse, and turning the wheel to port.

Accomplished   **Mentor signature_____   Date_____**

Name: _____

Task COX-03-03-AUX

Task	**State The Operational Limitations And Characteristics Of The Facility**
References	Boat Crew Seamanship Manual, COMDTINST M16114.5 (series), Chapter 2 and 8
	Auxiliary Operations Policy Manual, COMDTINST M16798.3 (series), Chapter 1
	Facility's Capacity Plate
Conditions	Performed at any time ashore, at the dock, or afloat. Trainee must accomplish task without prompting. Use of a reference is allowed.
Standards	In response to the mentor, the trainee must state the policy for operational limitations and review the operational limitations and specific characteristics of the facility being trained on.

Completed   **Performance Criteria**

_____ 1. Stated the policy requirements for the Director and active duty unit commanders to establish facility operational limitation standards.

_____ 2. Stated the policy requirements and responsibility of the coxswain concerning the facility's published operational limitations.

_____ 3. Stated the operational limitations for the facility established by the Director and/or operational commander. They must include the following:

     a. Minimum crew size for the facility.

     b. Maximum sea and wind state the facility can operate in.

     c. Maximum size and weight of a vessel that can be towed.

     d. Maximum sea conditions a vessel can be towed in.

     e. Distance offshore allowed during operations (if applicable).

Task COX-03-03-AUX (Continued)

_____ 4. Stated the facility's specific limitations including:

      a. Minimum crew size.

      b. Maximum number of personnel that can be carried on the facility.

      c. Maximum load capacity.

      d. Maximum speed of the facility.

      e. Maximum range at cruising speed, in nautical miles.

Accomplished   **Mentor signature**_____   **Date**_____

Name: _____

Task COX-03-04-AUX

Task	**Complete A Pre-Underway Check-Off For The Facility**
References	None
Conditions	Performed at the dock **AND** on the facility. Trainee must accomplish task with out prompting, and shall use the pre-underway check-off sheet as a reference. A diagram showing the location of equipment on the facility shall also be used.
Standards	In response to the mentor, the trainee must conduct a pre-underway check-off for the facility to locate and check proper condition, operation, and stowage of required equipment. Routine mechanical, electrical, and engine checks will also be done. The pre-underway check-off shall be performed using an up-to-date prepared checklist for the facility that covers the specific performance criteria listed below.

Completed   Performance Criteria

_____ 1. Verified appropriate Coast Guard patrol orders have been issued.

_____ 2. Confirmed with the operational commander or controlling authority the working radio frequency to be used for the mission and number of people on board (POB).

_____ 3. Located and checked the proper condition, operation, and stowage of the following equipment.

      _____a. Personal Floatation Devices (PFDs).

      _____b. Fire extinguishers.

      _____c. Visual distress signals.

      _____d. Anchors and anchor lines.

      _____e. Dewatering device.

      _____f. Watch or clock.

      _____g. Boarding ladder (or other means of boarding).

Task COX-03-04-AUX (Continued)

_____ h. Kicker/skiff hook (if required).

_____ i. Binoculars.

_____ j. Blanket.

_____ k. Fenders.

_____ l. Towline.

_____ m. Bridle.

_____ n. Heaving lines.

_____ o. Mooring lines.

_____ p. Searchlight.

_____ q. Spare navigation light bulbs.

_____ r. Boat hook.

_____ s. Navigation lights.

_____ t. Fathometer or sounding pole.

_____ u. Charts, navigation plotting instruments.

_____ v. Tools and spare parts.

_____ w. First aid kit.

_____ x. Sound producing device.

_____ y. Current Rules of the Road publication.

_____ 4. Completed the required mechanical, electrical, and engine checks listed below:

_____ a. Oil level (if applicable).

_____ b. Water level (if applicable).

_____ c. Reduction gear oil level (if applicable).

Task COX-03-04-AUX (Continued)

_____d. Fuel system, especially fuel shut off valves.

_____e. Ventilation system (if applicable).

_____ 5. Conducted crew briefing:

_____a. Purpose of mission.

_____b. Any special circumstances concerning the mission.

_____c. Working radio frequency to be used for the mission.

_____d. Expected weather and sea conditions.

_____e. Crewmembers in proper uniform and equipment.

_____f. Confirmed crewmembers are physically capable to perform mission.

_____g. Discussed and encouraged team coordination. Used the SPE, GAR, or other model to conduct a risk assessment of the patrol. Incorporated risk elements into pre-underway crew briefing.

_____h. Discussed the policy on wearing jewelry. Crew is in compliance.

_____ 6. Performed the following to prepare facility for getting underway:

_____a. Secured all openings.

_____b. Secured boat for sea (no loose gear).

_____c. Displayed proper flags and signboards.

_____d. Opened sea suction (if applicable).

_____e. Ventilated the engine compartment before starting engine(s).

_____f. Started the engine(s).

_____g. Engine/marine gear oil pressure satisfactory (if equipped).

_____h. Checked cooling water overboard discharge.

_____i. Energized the electrical and electronic systems (bilge pump, etc.).

Task COX-03-04-AUX (Continued)

_____j. Engine/marine gear oil pressure satisfactory (if equipped).

_____k. Disconnected shore tie(s).

_____ 7. Tested the following electronic equipment (if equipped):

_____a. VHF - FM radio(s).

_____b. Loud hailer.

_____c. Fathometer.

_____d. Loran C/GPS/DGPS.

_____e. RADAR

_____f. Chart Plotter

_____ 8. Tested engine controls in forward and reverse with lines still attached to the dock. Noted the reaction for both directions.

Accomplished **Mentor signature**_____ **Date**_____

Name. _____

Task COX-03-05-AUX

Task	**Get The Boat Away From The Dock**
References	Boat Crew Seamanship Manual, COMDTINST M16114.5 (series), Chapter 10
Conditions	Performed at the dock in calm sea and wind conditions. All mooring lines must be attached before task begins. Adjust operation for any wind or current.
Standards	In response to the mentor, the trainee must perform the steps listed below. Trainee must give verbal commands for all line handling procedures.

Completed	**Performance Criteria**
_____	1. Briefed the crew on the procedures to be used for getting underway and their assigned duties.
_____	2. Stated and compensated for the expected effects of the wind and current.
_____	3. Gave commands for all line handling in a loud/clear voice and acknowledged the responses of the crewmember(s).
_____	4. All lines brought aboard except the bow spring line (if needed).
_____	5. With the use of walking fenders, cleared stern of the boat by going ahead slowly and springing the stern out (if bow spring line used).
_____	6. Took in bow spring line when stern well clear of the dock.
_____	7. Boat was eased out from the dock until clear of all obstacles with room to move ahead.

Accomplished   Mentor signature_____ Date_____

Name: _____

Task COX-03-06-AUX

Task	**Operate The Boat And Apply Its Handling Characteristics In Following, Head And Beam Seas**
References	Boat Crew Seamanship Manual, COMDTINST M16114.5 (series), Chapter 10
Conditions	Performed during daylight in moderate sea conditions on a facility that is within its operational limitations for the conditions. If the above conditions are not available, seas may be created by another boat. Trainee must accomplish task without prompting or use of a reference.
Standards	In response to the mentor, the trainee must operate the facility in following, head, and beam seas, accomplishing the steps below without endangering personnel or the facility.

Completed   **Performance Criteria**

_____ 1. Stated the Coast Guard's policy on Auxiliary facilities operating in surf.

_____ 2. Stated why the facility should not routinely exceed 90% of its speed capability.

_____ 3. Briefed crew on the following:

   a. Cautioned crew to maintain a firm hold at all times and keep knees slightly flexed to help absorb shock.

   b. Discussed escape routes and procedures to follow in an emergency.

_____ 4. Operated the facility in following seas:

   a. Discussed corrective procedures to take if the boat begins surfing.

   b. Defined the term broaching and stated it primary cause.

Task COX-03-06-AUX (Continued)

   c. Operated the facility properly, maintaining the same speed as the seas and on the back of the swell. Avoided jumping over or riding on the front of a wave.

   d. DID NOT run directly before a swell. Kept heading at a slight angle (not more than 15 degrees), to the swell (seas on the quarter).

   e. Slowed down when necessary to allow overtaking seas to pass beneath the boat.

_____ 5. Operated the facility in head seas:

   a. Approached head seas at a slight angle, prepared to straighten boat out quickly to prevent a large wave from pushing boat broadside.

   b. Adjusted boat's speed as necessary to keep propellers in the water.

   c. Timed process through the seas so that the boat's bow rose to meet swells.

   d. Used only enough power to break through the crest; then cut back on power to let the boat fall on the backside of the swell.

   e. Boat's speed increased as swell approached (lifts bow) and avoided flying boat through the wave crest.

_____ 6. Operated facility in a beam seas:

   a. Avoided being broadside to heavy swells.

   b. Tacked facility across sea at a slight angle in a zigzag fashion and made each track as long as possible.

   c. Warned the crew when reversing course, then allowing boat to lose headway, applied hard rudder, and applied power.

Accomplished   Mentor signature_____ **Date**_____

Name: _____

Task COX-03-07-AUX

Task	**Maneuver A Boat In A Narrow Channel Or In A River (Waiverable By DIRAUX)**

References Boat Crew Seamanship Manual, COMDTINST M16114.5 (series), Chapter 10

Conditions Performed underway on a facility, during daylight, in good weather and calm seas conditions. This task will be accomplished while transiting parallel to the banks of a river, a narrow channel or seawall with limited maneuverability where bank cushion and bank suction may be expected. Trainee must accomplish task without prompting or use of a reference. Trainee will operate the facility and do all maneuvers.

Standards In response to the mentor, the trainee must use the boat's propeller, rudder action, and handling characteristics in combination with the existing current velocity and direction to obtain the best advantage in controlling and maneuvering the facility and must station-keep and turn the facility 180 degrees within the confines of a narrow channel, harbor entrance, or inlet in accordance with the steps below. Trainee must perform the task without endangering personnel or the facility.

NOTE: May be waived by the Director in accordance with Section 1.B.4.

Completed   **Performance Criteria**

_____ 1. Briefed the crew on procedures to be used and their duties.

_____ 2. Anticipated and explained the predicted effects of the wind on the maneuvering of the facility.

_____ 3. Defined bank cushion and stated its effect on boat handling/maneuvering.

_____ 4. Defined bank suction and stated its effect on boat handling/maneuvering.

_____ 5. Stated when "bank cushion" and "bank suction" would be the strongest and weakest when turning in a sharp bend in a narrow channel.

_____ 6. Maintained position (station-keeping) in the center of the channel for at least three minutes.

Task COX-03-07-AUX (Continued)

_____ 7. Brought the facility around in the channel from a "facing the current" (up current) position to a "with the current" (down current) position.

_____ 8. Brought the facility around in the channel from a "with the current" (down current), position to a "facing the current" (up current) position.

_____ 9. Maneuvered the facility in a narrow channel under the following conditions:

      a. straight channel

      b. passing another boat

      c. turning in a bend, against the current (middle of channel)

      d. turning in a bend, going with the current

      e. hugging the point

      f. staying in the bend

      g. staying on bend side, middle of channel

Accomplished   Mentor signature_____   **Date**_____

Name: _____

Task COX-03-08-AUX

Task	**Maneuver The Boat Alongside Another Boat With No Way On**
References	Boat Crew Seamanship Manual, COMDTINST M16114.5 (series), Chapter 10
Conditions	Performed while underway on a facility in calm sea conditions. Trainee must accomplish task without prompting or use of a reference.
Standards	In response to the mentor, the trainee must maneuver the facility in accordance with the steps below.

Completed   **Performance Criteria**

_____   1. Brief the crew and assigned duties.

_____   2. Established communications with the other boat.

_____   3. Briefed personnel on the other boat.

_____   4. Rigged fenders. Walking fender available if needed.

_____   5. Made approach to other boat.

_____   6. Brought Auxiliary facility alongside other boat.

_____   7. Maneuvered Auxiliary facility away from other boat.

Accomplished   **Mentor signature**_____   **Date**_____

Name: _____

Task COX-03-9-AUX

Task	**Moor The Boat To A Dock**
References	Boat Crew Seamanship Manual, COMDTINST M16114.5 (series), Chapter 10
Conditions	Performed underway on a facility in calm wind and sea conditions. Trainee must be at the helm as the Coxswain and must accomplish task without prompting or use of a reference.
Standards	In response to the mentor, the trainee must moor the facility to a dock in accordance with the steps below. Coxswain trainee must give verbal commands for all line handling procedures.

Completed   **Performance Criteria**

_____   1. Briefed the crew on procedures to be used and their duties.

_____   2. Stated the expected effects of the wind and current on mooring the facility.

_____   3. Approached the dock slowly at an angle.

_____   4. Directed crew to secure the after bow spring line (#2 line) when the bow was alongside the intended mooring point on the dock. Applied full rudder away from the dock, stern sprung, or pivoted toward dock.

_____   5. Directed crew to secure stern line (#4 line) then the remaining lines (#1 line and #3 line).

_____   6. Ensured that all mooring lines were adjusted for expected tidal changes and wave/wake action.

Accomplished   **Mentor signature**_____ **Date**_____

Name: _____

Task COX-03-10-AUX

Task	**Anchor The Boat**
References	Boat Crew Seamanship Manual, COMDTINST M16114.5 (series), Chapter 10
Conditions	Performed underway on a facility in calm wind and sea conditions during daylight. Trainee must be at the helm as the Coxswain and accomplish task without prompting or use of a reference.
Standards	In response to the mentor, the trainee must anchor the facility in accordance with the steps below. Coxswain trainee must give verbal commands for all line handling procedures. Tasks must be accomplished without endangering personnel or the boat. Facility must be anchored with room to swing.

Completed   **Performance Criteria**

_____ 1. Selected and plotted position for placement of the anchor noting the depth of water, bottom contours, and characteristics.

_____ 2. Briefed crew on anchoring procedure. Assigned duties and reviewed hand signals to be used.

_____ 3. Piloted boat to selected position.

_____ 4. Described expected effects of wind and current on anchoring the boat.

_____ 5. Determined approximate length of the scope (rode) by checking depth of water, adding boat's freeboard at the bow and room available for the boat to swing.

_____ 6. Directed crew to rig anchor and prepare for anchoring.

_____ 7. Approached anchorage keeping boat headed into the wind and/or current.

_____ 8. Checked boat's headway at the charted anchoring position.

Task COX-03-10-AUX (Continued)

_____ 9. Directed crew to LOWER (NOT THROW) the anchor to the bottom with a round turn on bitt/cleat.

_____ 10. Backed boat down away from the anchor with the crew slowly paying out the anchor line until proper scope reached.

_____ 11. Directed crew to make anchor line fast to bitt/cleat with a round turn and figure eights.

_____ 12. Fixed actual position using three visual or radar bearings.

_____ 13. Checked water depth using fathometer, lead line, or sounding pole.

_____ 14. Ensured anchor was not dragging.

_____ 15. Set anchor watch, briefed watch on responsibilities.

Accomplished   **Mentor signature**_____   **Date**_____

Name: _____

Task COX-03-11-AUX

Task	**Weigh The Boat's Anchor**
References	Boat Crew Seamanship Manual, COMDTINST M16114.5 (series), Chapter 10
Conditions	Performed underway on a facility in calm wind and sea conditions during daylight. Trainee must accomplish task without prompting or use of a reference.
Standards	In response to the mentor, the trainee must weigh the anchor of the facility in accordance with the steps below. Coxswain trainee must give verbal commands for all line handling procedures. Tasks must be accomplished without endangering personnel or boat.

Completed   **Performance Criteria**

_____ 1. Briefed crew on anchoring procedure to be used. Defined their duties and what hand signals will be used, emphasized safety.

_____ 2. Moved boat ahead slowly, using engine(s).

_____ 3. Directed crew to take up slack in the anchor line as boat moved forward to prevent fouling screw(s). Faked the anchor line out of the way IMMEDIATELY or rewound on reel.

_____ 4. Attempted to retrieve anchor when anchor line was tending up and down (vertical).

_____ 5. If the anchor failed to break free:

        a. Directed crewmember to make the anchor line fast around the forward bitt/cleat.

        b. Maneuvered boat ahead a few feet after anchor line made fast.

        c. If anchor not freed, placed engine(s) ahead slow and maneuvered in a wide circle until anchor freed.

_____ 6. Made up and secured all gear.

Accomplished   **Mentor signature**_____   **Date**_____

Section D.   Rules Of The Road

Introduction	The following are the objectives of Section D:

- **Display competence** in the knowledge and use of the International-Inland Rules of the Road

- **Demonstrate** knowledge of various sound signals used while underway

- **Demonstrate** knowledge of various light configurations used while underway.

In this section   This section contains three tasks.

Reading Assignments	Task Number	Task	See Page
Ref (e)	COX-04-01-AUX	Successfully Complete The Navigation Rules Of The Road Exam	2-35
Ref (e) Part D	COX-04-02-AUX	Execute Commonly Used Sound Signals	2-36
Ref (e) Part C	COX-04-03-AUX	Set The Proper Navigation Lights For Common Operational Evolutions	2-38

Name: _____

Task COX-04-01-AUX

Task	**Successfully Complete The Navigation Rules Of The Road Exam**

References Navigation Rules Inland-International, COMDTINST M16672.2 (series)

Auxiliary Boat Crew Training Manual, COMDTINST M16794.51 (series)

Conditions Task must be performed at any time in a manner prescribed by the above references and the course or examination issuing authority.

Standards Trainee must receive a passing score (90%) on the Auxiliary Navigation Rules Examination—Initial Qualification (closed book), **or** pass the Coast Guard Institute's NAVRULS End of Course Test or Deck Watch Officer Examination. A QE must verify by checking one of the below and signing the task.

Completed   **Performance Criteria**

_____ 1. Passed the Auxiliary Navigation Rules Examination - Initial Qualification, **or**

_____ 2. Passed the Coast Guard Institute's NAVRULS End of Course Test or Deck Watch Officer Examination.

Accomplished **QE signature** _____ _____ **Date** _____

Name: _____

Task COX-04-02-AUX

Task	**Execute Commonly Used Sound Signals**
References	Navigation Rules Inland-International, COMDTINST M16672.2 (series), Part D
Conditions	Performed by manually operating the boat's horn or fog signal. May be done at the dock or underway, day or night, in any weather. Signals under international and/or inland rules should be demonstrated depending on which rules normally apply in the trainee's operating area.
Standards	In response to the mentor, the trainee must demonstrate the proper sound signals as listed below. **NOTE: When performing the task, care must be exercised to avoid confusing boats underway in the immediate vicinity.**

Completed   Performance Criteria

_____   1. Activated horn manually.

_____   2. Demonstrated short blast.

_____   3. Demonstrated prolonged blast.

_____   4. Sounded signal for action or intention and answer for a boat altering course to starboard or passing port to port.

_____   5. Sounded signal for action or intention and answer for a boat altering course to port or passing starboard to starboard.

_____   6. Sounded signal for operating astern propulsion.

_____   7. Sounded signal for overtaking and passing another boat on the starboard side.

_____   8. Sounded signal for overtaking and passing another boat on the port side.

Task COX-04-02-AUX (Continued)

_____ 9. Sounded signal for avoiding collision, or when failing to understand the action/intention of another boat (danger signal).

_____ 10. Sounded signal for power driven boat underway with way on in restricted visibility.

_____ 11. Sounded signal for power driven boat underway with no way on in restricted visibility.

_____ 12. Sounded signal for boat not under command or with restricted maneuverability in restricted visibility.

_____ 13. Sounded signal for boat with stern tow in restricted visibility.

_____ 14. Sounded signal for boat being towed astern in restricted visibility.

_____ 15. Sounded signal for boat at anchor in restricted visibility.

Accomplished **Mentor signature**_____ **Date**_____

Name: _____

Task COX-04-03-AUX

Task	**Set The Proper Navigation Lights For Common Operational Boat Evolutions**
References	Navigation Rules Inland-International, COMDTINST M16672.2 (series), Part C
Conditions	Task may be done at the dock or underway, day or night, on an Auxiliary Facility. Light displays should be for either international or inland rules, depending on which rules normally apply in the trainee's operating area. Trainee must accomplish task without prompting or use of a reference.
Standards	In response to the mentor, the trainee must energize and set the proper lights in accordance with the steps listed below. Lights must be proper for the situation, size and type of boat they are displayed on.

Completed   **Performance Criteria**

_____   1. Proper light displayed for vessel underway.

_____   2. Proper light displayed for vessel anchored.

_____   3. Proper lights displayed or explained for towing a vessel astern.

_____   4. Properly lights displayed or explained for towing a vessel alongside.

Accomplished   **Mentor signature**_____   **Date**_____

Section E.   Piloting And Navigation

Introduction

The following are the objectives of Section E:

- **Identify** and **state** the use of various common navigational references.

- **Demonstrate** the ability to pilot using installed electronic navigational equipment.

- **Demonstrate** the ability to pilot a boat using dead reckoning techniques

- **Demonstrate** a knowledge of the local operating area

In this section

This section contains eleven tasks:

Reading Assignments	Task Number	Task	See Page
Ref (b) Chapter 14, Section D	COX-05-01-AUX	Identify Navigational Publications	2-40
Ref (b) Chapter 14, Section D	COX-05-02-AUX	Obtain A Visual Fix	2-41
Ref (b) Chapter 14, Section C	COX-05-03-AUX	Determine A Compass Course For True Course	2-42
None	COX-05-04-AUX	Sketch A Chart Of The Local Operating Area	2-43
Ref (b) Chapter 14, Section D	COX-05-05-AUX	Pilot A Boat Using Dead Reckoning Techniques	2-44
Ref (b) Chapter 14, Section D	COX-05-06-AUX	Pilot A Boat Using "Seaman's Eye"	2-45
Radar User Manual Ref (b) Chapter 14, Section D	COX-05-07-AUX	Determine The Position Of A Boat Using Radar Ranges And Bearing (If Equipped)	2-46
GPS User Manual Ref (b) Chapter 14, Section D	COX-05-08-AUX	Determine The Position Of A Boat Using GPS/DGPS (If Equipped)	2-47
LORAN C User Manual Ref (b) Chapter 14, Section D	COX-05-09-AUX	Determine The Position Of A Boat Using LORAN C (If Equipped)	2-48
Ref (b) Chapter 14, Section D	COX-05-10-AUX	Determine Course To Steer And Speed Over Ground (SOG) Allowing For Set And Drift	2-49
Ref (b) Chapter 14, Section E	COX-05-11-AUX	River Sailing (Locks, Dams And Flood Warnings) And Pass Through A Lock **(Waiverable by DIRAUX)**	2-51

Name: _____

Task COX-05-01-AUX

Task	**Identify Navigational Publications**
References	Boat Crew Seamanship Manual, COMDTINST M16114.5 (series), Chapter 14
Conditions	Performed at any time ashore, at the dock, or afloat. Trainee must accomplish task without prompting or use of a reference.
Standards	In response to the mentor, the trainee must identify the navigational publications listed below and state their purpose.

Completed   **Performance Criteria**

_____   1. Identified the Navigation Rules International-Inland, COMDTINST M16672.2 (series), and stated its use.

_____   2. Identified a Coast Pilot and stated its use. Was familiar with local entries.

_____   3. Identified a Light List and stated its use. Was familiar with local entries.

_____   4. Identified a Local Notice to Mariners and stated its use.

_____   5. Identified Tide Tables (where applicable) and stated their use. Was familiar with local entries.

_____   6. Identified Tidal Current Tables (where applicable) and stated their use. Was familiar with local entries.

Accomplished   **Mentor signature**_____   **Date**_____

Name: _____

Task COX-05-02-AUX

Task	**Obtain A Visual Fix**
References	Boat Crew Seamanship Manual, COMDTINST M16114.5 (series), Chapter 14
Conditions	Performed underway in fair weather, in calm, or moderate seas. The mentor will provide the trainee with at least three visual objects from which to determine compass bearings. Bearings may be determined using either a hand bearing compass or by sighting over the boats's navigational compass. A nautical chart covering the operating area, pencil and paper, parallel rules/plotter, and a deviation table are necessary to perform task. Trainee must accomplish task without prompting or use of a reference.
Standards	In response to the mentor, the trainee must show proficiency in correctly obtaining and plotting a visual fix on a chart.

Completed   **Performance Criteria**

_____   1. Obtained compass course and selected objects from which to determine magnetic bearings for plotting from the mentor.

_____   2. Plotted the compass course and labeled "course" along the top of the line and "speed" below it.

_____   3. Determined the compass bearing of the first object.

_____   4. Converted the compass bearing to magnetic bearing.

_____   5. Repeat steps 3 and 4 for remaining objects.

_____   6. Plotted the magnetic bearing of both objects on the chart, labeled the bearings with the time along the top of the lines and bearing below the lines.

_____   7. Labeled the fix where the Lines of Position (LOPs) intersect with a dot enclosed by a circle with the time followed with the letters "VIS FIX" to the side of the circle at an angle clear of the course line.

_____   8. Verified depth by fathometer.

Accomplished   **Mentor signature**_____   **Date**_____

Name: _____

Task COX-05-03-AUX

Task	**Determine Compass Course From True Course**
References	Boat Crew Seamanship Manual, COMDTINST M16114.5 (series), Chapter 14
	Auxiliary facility's current deviation table
Conditions	Performed at any time ashore, at the dock, or afloat. Given a nautical chart of the local operating area, the facility's deviation table, and 3 true courses, by the mentor, the trainee must show proficiency in chart plotting. Trainee must accomplish task without prompting or use of a reference.
Standards	In response to the mentor, the trainee must, without error, convert three given TRUE courses into COMPASS courses and plot on a chart.

Completed   **Performance Criteria**

_____   1. Stated the magnetic variation for the local area found on the compass rose.

_____   2. Identified and stated the use of the facility's deviation table.

_____   3. Plotted and labeled true courses identified by the mentor.

_____   4. Determined magnetic course for each true course.

_____   5. Determined compass courses for each magnetic course.

_____   6. Correctly plotted and labeled each compass course on the chart.

Accomplished   **Mentor signature**_____   **Date**_____

Name: _____

Task COX-05-04-AUX

Task   **Sketch A Chart Of The Local Operating Area**

References   Local charts and personal knowledge of the local area

Conditions   Performed at any time ashore, at the dock, or afloat. Sketch on a plain sheet of paper. Trainee must accomplish task without prompting or use of a reference.

Standards   In response to the mentor, the trainee must sketch and label from memory a chart of the local operating area. The sketch does not have to be to scale but should approximate relative distances and shapes. The mentor shall approve the area to be sketched.

Completed   **Performance Criteria**

_____   1. Sketched and labeled the local operating area.

_____   2. Sketched prominent coast lines noting the following, as appropriate:

        a. Points

        b. Capes

        c. Harbors and local basins

        d. Landmarks

_____   3. Sketched major hazards to navigation (wrecks, rocks, shoals, bars, submerged pilings, fishnet areas, etc.).

_____   4. Sketched shipping and boat channels.

Accomplished   **Mentor signature**_____   **Date**_____

Name: _____

Task COX-05-05-AUX

Task	**Pilot A Boat Using Dead Reckoning Techniques**
References	Boat Crew Seamanship Manual, COMDTINST M16114.5 (series), Chapter 14
Conditions	Performed underway on a facility during daylight, in calm to moderate weather conditions, using only the installed compass, speed/engine RPM curve, stop watch, navigational kit, and charts found on the facility. The course must be at least 3 miles long with at least two turns. All courses and speeds to turn points are to be given to the trainee by the mentor. Trainee must accomplish task without prompting or use of a reference.
Standards	In response to the mentor, the trainee must perform tasks. Turn points must be determined using the most accurate method available to the boat. All plotting on charts must be done using proper chart notation and symbols. All locations must be verified by taking a simultaneous sounding using the fathometer, if available. All locations should be verified by the mentor.

Completed   **Performance Criteria**

_____   1. Compass course laid out on the chart indicating predicted turns.

_____   2. ETA to first turn point predicted and facility piloted to the first predicted position using only boat's compass, speed/engine RPM curve and stop watch.

_____   3. ETA to next turn point predicted with course and speed corrected to make good the second position.

_____   4. Facility piloted to the next predicted position using only boat's compass, speed/engine RPM curve, and stop watch.

_____   5. Step 4 and 5 repeated until voyage was completed.

Accomplished   **Mentor signature**_____   **Date**_____

Name: _____

Task COX-05-06-AUX

Task	**Pilot A Boat Using "Seaman's Eye"**
References	Boat Crew Seamanship Manual, COMDTINST M16114.5 (series), Chapter 14
Conditions	Task must be performed while underway, in calm weather conditions. Task should run over a course provided by the mentor of at least 3 nautical miles and containing at least 8 course changes, using only a local chart of the area, local knowledge of the area, aids to navigation, terrestrial landmarks, and "Seaman's Eye." Visibility must be at least 1 nautical mile. Trainee must accomplish the task without prompting or use of any reference.
Standards	Course must be steered directly without wandering or requiring any stopping or backtracking in order to stay on course or within any channels. At no time may the vessel or crew be put in danger.

Completed   **Performance Criteria**

_____   1. Laid out and labeled the courses on the chart.

_____   2. Cleared the pier/dock and started on course.

_____   3. Identified terrestrial landmark or aids to navigation to be used to steer to first turn point.

_____   4. Steered boat directly to first turn point.

_____   5. Turned boat upon reaching first turn point.

_____   6. Identified terrestrial landmark or aids to navigation to be used to steer to second turn point.

_____   7. Steered boat directly to next turn point.

_____   8. Repeated steps 5-7 until voyage was completed.

Accomplished   Mentor signature_____   Date_____

Name: _____

Task COX-05-07-AUX

Task   **Determine The Position Of A Boat Using Radar Ranges And Bearings (If Equipped)**

References   Boat Crew Seamanship Manual, COMDTINST M16114.5 (series), Chapter 14

Conditions   Performed underway in calm to moderate weather, using installed radar, compass, fathometer, navigation kit, and charts found on the facility; chart should be a harbor chart or some other large scale chart.

Standards   In response to the mentor, the trainee must perform tasks. Correctly plot positions within one tenth of a nautical mile. All plotting should be done using proper chart notation and symbols. If available, all positions are to be verified by taking a simultaneous sounding using the fathometer.

Completed   **Performance Criteria**

_____   1. Activated and properly tuned radar set.

_____   2. Determined position of the boat underway, but with no way on.

_____   3. Determined position of the boat underway at slow speed.

_____   4. Determined position of the boat using ranges.

_____   5. Determined position of the boat using bearings.

_____   6. Verified all positions by using the fathometer to check soundings (if equipped).

Accomplished   **Mentor signature**_____   **Date**_____

Name: _____

Task COX-05-08-AUX

Task	**Determine The Position Of A Boat Using GPS/DPGS (If Equipped)**
References	Boat Crew Seamanship Manual, COMDTINST M16114.5 (series), Chapter 14
Conditions	Performed underway using the installed GPS, navigational kit, and charts found on the facility.
Standards	In response to the mentor, the trainee must perform tasks. Correctly plot 2 positions of the boat to an accuracy of one tenth of a nautical mile. All plotting should be done using proper chart notation and symbols. The mentor should verify positions.

Completed   **Performance Criteria**

_____   1. Activated GPS.

_____   2. Plotted position of the boat on a chart, using latitude and longitude reading obtained from the boat's GPS.

_____   3. Verified all positions by using the fathometer, if available.

Accomplished   **Mentor signature**_____   **Date**_____

Name: _____

Task COX-05-09-AUX

Task	**Determine The Position Of A Boat Using LORAN C (If Equipped)**
References	Boat Crew Seamanship Manual, COMDTINST M16114.5 (series), Chapter 14
Conditions	Performed underway using the installed LORAN C, navigational kit, and charts found on the facility.
Standards	In response to the mentor, the trainee must perform tasks. Correctly plot 2 positions of the boat to an accuracy of one tenth of a nautical mile. All plotting should be done using proper chart notation and symbols. The mentor should verify positions.

Completed	**Performance Criteria**
_____	1. Activated and properly tuned LORAN C unit.
_____	2. Identified master and secondary signals for unit's local operating area.
_____	3. Plotted position of the boat on a chart, using latitude and longitude reading.
_____	4. Plotted position of the boat on a chart, using time difference lines (TD) obtained from the LORAN C unit.
_____	5. Verified positions using the fathometer, if available.

Accomplished   **Mentor signature**_____   **Date**_____

Name: _____

Task COX-05-10-AUX

Task	**Determine Course To Steer And Speed Over Ground (SOG) Allowing For Set And Drift**
References	Boat Crew Seamanship Manual, COMDTINST M16114.5 (series), Chapter 14
Conditions	Performed both ashore and while underway. The underway portion will be performed in daylight in fair weather conditions, in calm or moderate seas. The mentor will provide the trainee with intended course and designated speed for the boat. Navigational tools, chart, and appropriate volume of the Tidal Current Tables will be required.
Standards	In response to the mentor, the trainee must plot the current triangle on the chart's compass rose. True direction must be used for plotting the current. The intended course, current direction, and course to steer must be plotted within three degrees. Speed will be determined to the nearest tenth of a knot. After determination of a true course to steer, convert to compass course for small boat navigation and state the basic concepts related to navigation as outlined in the steps below.

Completed   **Performance Criteria**

_____   1. Defined the terms set and drift associated with current.

_____   2. Stated the causes of set and drift.

_____   3. Stated the three vectors represented by the current triangle.

_____   4. Obtained the intended course and designated speed of the boat from the mentor.

_____   5. Used the center of the compass rose as departure point, drew boat's intended course through the center of the compass rose. Made this line indefinite in length. This is the desired course and speed vector.

_____   6. Obtained from the Tidal Current Table the true direction and speed of the current. Drew line for true direction of the current from the center of the compass rose; made line the length of the current's speed (one knot is equal to one nautical mile) and placed an arrowhead at the outer end of the line. This is the set and drift vector. Measurement can be made with dividers either from the nautical mile or latitude scale on the chart.

Task COX-05-10-AUX (Continued)

_____ 7. Used dividers to measure the designated speed of the boat along the desired course line drawn in STEP #6. Placed a small arrowhead at this point and a drew small circle around it.

_____ 8. Drew a straight line to connect the arrow point of the direction and speed of current, (set and drift vector). This line is the <u>course to steer</u> and <u>speed over ground (SOG)</u> needed to achieve the desired course and speed. Measured the length of this line to obtain boat speed to run.

_____ 9. Converted true course to compass course for small boat navigation.

Accomplished **Mentor signature**_____ **Date**_____

Name: _____

Task COX-05-11-AUX

Task **River Sailing, (Locks, Dams and Flood Warnings), And Pass Through A Lock (Waiverable by DIRAUX)**

References Boat Crew Seamanship Manual, COMDTINST M16114.5 (series), Chapter 14

Conditions Performed underway in calm wind and sea conditions, during the daylight. Trainee must accomplish task without prompting or use of a reference.

Standards In response to the mentor, the trainee must show knowledge of locks, dams, and flood warnings and operate the facility through a lock.

NOTE: May be waived by the Director in accordance with Section 1.B.4.

Completed **Performance Criteria**

_____ 1. Stated understanding of locks and dams construction and operation.

_____ 2. Stated understanding of locking procedures and signals.

   a. Stated Lock Master's authority

   b. Stated lock priority for pleasure craft

   c. Identified and used proper radio frequency guarded by the Lock Master

   d. Followed sound and light signals at the locks

_____ 3. Directed crew to rig fenders, break out mooring lines, and tend while pasing through the lock.

_____ 4. Stated understanding of safety considerations navigating around dams.

_____ 5. Stated understanding of flood warnings.

Accomplished **Mentor signature_____ Date_____**

Section F.   Search And Rescue

Introduction

The following are the objectives for Section F:

- **Demonstrate** knowledge of SAR organization and responsibility.

- **Demonstrate** knowledge of SAR fundamentals.

- **Demonstrate** the ability to plot and execute commonly used search patterns.

In this section

This section contains ten tasks:

Reading Assignments	Task Number	Task	See Page
Ref (b) Chapter 15, Section A	COX-06-01-AUX	Organization And Responsibility	2-53
Ref (b) Chapter 15, Section C Ref (d) Chapter 4, Section E Ref (f) Chapter 4, Section 4.1 and 4.2	COX-06-02-AUX	Legal Aspects And USCG Policy	2-54
Ref (b) Chapter 15, Section B Ref (f) Chapter 4, Section 4.2	COX-06-03-AUX	SAR Emergency Phases	2-56
Ref (d) Chapter 15, Section E Ref (f) Appendix H	COX-06-04-AUX	State The Basic Concepts Related To Search Planning	2-57
Ref (d) Chapter 15, Section E Ref (f) Appendix H, Section H.7	COX-06-05-AUX	Plot A Single Unit Expanding Square Search Pattern (SS)	2-59
Ref (d) Chapter 15, Section E Ref (f) Appendix H, Section H.7	COX-06-06-AUX	Plot A Single Unit Sector Search Pattern (VS)	2-60
Ref (d) Chapter 15, Section E Ref (f) Appendix H, Section H.7	COX-06-07-AUX	Plot A Single Unit Parallel Search Pattern (PS)	2-61
Ref (d) Chapter 15, Section E Ref (f) Appendix H, Section H.7	COX-06-08-AUX	Plot A Single Unit Trackline Return Search Pattern (TSR)	2-62
Ref (b) Chapter 15, Section F&G Ref (f) Appendix H, Section H.7	COX-06-09-AUX	Execute A Search Pattern	2-63
Ref (b) Chapter 11, Section B&F	COX-06-10-AUX	Obtain Distress Information And Pass To The Controlling Shore Unit	2-65

Name: _____

Task COX-06-01-AUX

Task	**Organization And Responsibility**
References	Boat Crew Seamanship Manual, COMDTINST M16114.5 (series), Chapter 15
Conditions	Performed at any time ashore, at the dock, or afloat. Trainee must accomplish task without prompting or use of a reference.
Standards	In response to the mentor, the trainee must state the basic concepts related to searching as outlined in the steps below.

Completed	**Performance Criteria**
_____	1. Stated the Coast Guard's geographic areas of responsibility for SAR.
_____	2. Stated the duties and responsibilities of the SAR Mission Coordinator.
_____	3. Stated the duties and responsibilities of the On Scene Commander.
_____	4. Stated the duties and responsibilities of the Search and Rescue Unit.

Accomplished   **Mentor signature**_____   **Date**_____

Name. _____

Task COX-06-02-AUX

Task	**Legal Aspects And USCG Policies**
References	Boat Crew Seamanship Manual, COMDTINST M16114.5 (series), Chapter 15
	U.S. Coast Guard Addendum to the United States National Search and Rescue Supplement (NSS) to the International Aeronautical and Maritime Search and Rescue Manual (IAMSAR), COMDTINST M16130.2 (series), Chapter 4
	Auxiliary Operations Policy Manual, COMDTINST M16798.3 (series), Chapter 4
Conditions	Performed at any time ashore, at the dock, or afloat. Trainee must accomplish task without prompting or use of a reference.
Standards	In response to the mentor, the trainee must demonstrate a basic understanding of the legal aspects, USCG policy including Maritime SAR Assistance and General Salvage policy, and how it is related to Auxiliary SAR operations.

Completed	Performance Criteria
_____	1. Stated importance of distress beacons.
_____	2. Stated importance of flare sightings.
_____	3. Stated understanding of hoaxes and false alarms and the difference between them.
_____	4. Defined the Distress emergency phase of a SAR case.
_____	5. Defined a non-distress case.
_____	6. Discussed Coast Guard policy on responding to all requests for assistance, including "come upons."
_____	7. Stated resources the Coast Guard may use to provide assistance to boaters.

Task COX-06-02-AUX (Continued)

_____ 8. Stated actions Auxiliarists can take in cases determined to be in the Distress emergency phase.

_____ 9. Stated actions Auxiliarists can take in cases determined to be non-distress.

_____ 10. Stated actions a coxswain would perform when a disabled boat, not in contact with the Coast Guard, is found.

_____ 11. Defined Marine Assistance Request Broadcast (MARB) and described how it relates to Auxiliary SAR operations.

_____ 12. Stated when Coast Guard or Auxiliary units could engage in general salvage other than towing.

_____ 13. Stated what actions Auxiliarists under orders would take in responding to a mariner's request to refloat a grounded boat.

Accomplished **Mentor signature**_____ **Date**_____

Name: _____

Task COX-06-03-AUX

Task | **SAR Emergency Phases**

References | Boat Crew Seamanship Manual, COMDTINST M16114.5 (series), Chapter 15

U.S. Coast Guard Addendum to the United States National Search and Rescue Supplement (NSS) to the International Aeronautical and Maritime Search and Rescue Manual (IAMSAR), COMDTINST M16130.2 (series), Chapter 4

Conditions | Performed at any time ashore, at the dock, or afloat. Trainee must accomplish task without prompting or use of a reference.

Standards | In response to the mentor, the trainee must, without error, state the basic concepts related to searching as outlined in the steps below.

Completed | **Performance Criteria**

_____ 1. Defined the three phases of a SAR incident.

    a. Uncertainty phase

    b. Alert phase

    c. Distress phase

_____ 2. Stated the initial action to take for each phase of a SAR incident.

Accomplished   **Mentor signature**_____ **Date**_____

Name: _____

Task COX-06-04-AUX

Task	**State The Basic Concepts Related To Search Planning**
References	Boat Crew Seamanship Manual, COMDTINST M16114.5 (series), Chapter 15
	U.S. Coast Guard Addendum to the United States National Search and Rescue Supplement (NSS) to the International Aeronautical and Maritime Search and Rescue Manual (IAMSAR), COMDTINST M16130.2 (series), Appendix H
Conditions	Performed at any time ashore, at the dock, or afloat. Trainee must accomplish task without prompting or use of a reference.
Standards	In response to the mentor, the trainee must state the basic concepts related to searching as outlined in the steps below.

Completed   **Performance Criteria**

_____   1. Defined datum.

_____   2. Defined commence search point (CSP).

_____   3. Defined corner point search area description.

_____   4. Defined center point search area description.

_____   5. Defined boundary method search area description.

_____   6. Defined track spacing (TS).

_____   7. Stated items included on a pre-search check list.

_____   8. Described the following search patterns, both single unit (S) and multi unit (M), and described the conditions in which they are most likely to be used.

        a. Expanding Square (SS)

        b. Sector Search (VS)

Task COX-06-04-AUX (Continued)

    c. Parallel Search (PS)

    d. Creeping Line Search (CS)

    e. Trackline Single-Unit Return (TSR)

    f. Barrier Search (XSB)

    g. Initial Response Search area

Accomplished   **Mentor signature**_____   **Date**_____

Name: _____

Task COX-06-05-AUX

Task	**Plot A Single Unit Expanding Square Search Pattern (SS)**
References	Boat Crew Seamanship Manual, COMDTINST M16114.5 (series), Chapter 15
	U.S. Coast Guard Addendum to the United States National Search and Rescue Supplement (NSS) to the International Aeronautical and Maritime Search and Rescue Manual (IAMSAR), COMDTINST M16130.2 (series), Appendix H
Conditions	Performed at any time ashore. The mentor will provide the trainee with a Search Action Plan consisting of: Area Description (center point method), pattern designation, Commence Search Point (CSP), Track Spacing (TS), orientation of the first search leg, and search speed to be used. The first leg of the search should run in the direction of drift. All turns are made 90 degrees to the right. Trainee must accomplish task without prompting or use of a reference.
Standards	Tasks COX-06-05-AUX through COX-06-09-AUX cover the plotting of five search patterns. The trainee will select three and plot **three** of these patterns, based on appropriateness of the patterns for the type of facility and the needs of the operating area.
	In response to the mentor, the trainee will plot an SS search pattern with a minimum of five legs. Commence search point must be accurate to within 100 yards, track lines must be within 3 degrees, and times to run within 60 seconds.

Completed	**Performance Criteria**
_____	1. Correctly laid out search area and pattern on chart with the CSP in the proper location and the first search leg oriented in the direction of drift.
_____	2. Correctly calculated time to complete the search and the time to turn each search leg.

Accomplished   Mentor signature_____   Date_____

Name: _____

Task COX-06-06-AUX

Task	**Plot A Single Unit Sector Search Pattern (VS)**
References	Boat Crew Seamanship Manual, COMDTINST M16114.5 (series), Chapter 15
	U.S. Coast Guard Addendum to the United States National Search and Rescue Supplement (NSS) to the International Aeronautical and Maritime Search and Rescue Manual (IAMSAR), COMDTINST M16130.2 (series), Appendix H
Conditions	Performed at any time ashore. The mentor will provide trainee with a Search Action Plan consisting of: area description (<u>center point method</u>), pattern designation, Commence Search Point (CSP), orientation of the first search leg, and search speed.
Standards	Tasks COX-06-05-AUX through COX-06-09-AUX cover the plotting of five search patterns. The trainee will select three and plot **three** of these patterns, based on appropriateness of the patterns for the type of facility and the needs of the operating area.
	In response to the mentor, the trainee will plot a complete VS search pattern. All turns must be 120 degrees to the right. Commence search point must be accurate to within 100 yards, track lines must be within 3 degrees, and times to run within 60 seconds.

Completed	**Performance Criteria**
_____	1. Correctly laid out search area and pattern on chart with CSP in the proper location and the first search leg oriented in the direction of drift.
_____	2. Correctly calculated time to complete the search and time to turn each search leg.

Accomplished   Mentor signature_____   Date_____

Name: _____

Task COX-06-07-AUX

Task	**Plot A Single Unit Parallel Search (PS)**

References   Boat Crew Seamanship Manual, COMDTINST M16114.5 (series), Chapter 15

U.S. Coast Guard Addendum to the United States National Search and Rescue Supplement (NSS) to the International Aeronautical and Maritime Search and Rescue Manual (IAMSAR), COMDTINST M16130.2 (series), Appendix H

Conditions   Performed at any time ashore. The mentor will provide trainee with a Search Action Plan consisting of: area description (corner point method), pattern designation, Commence Search Point (CSP), Track Spacing and search speed.

Standards   Tasks COX-06-05-AUX through COX-06-09-AUX cover the plotting of five search patterns. The trainee will select three and plot **three** of these patterns, based on appropriateness of the patterns for the type of facility and the needs of the operating area.

In response to the mentor, the trainee will plot a PS pattern with a minimum of 6 legs. Commence search point must be accurate to within 100 yards, track lines must be within 3 degrees, and times to run within 60 seconds.

Completed   **Performance Criteria**

_____   1. Correctly laid out search area and pattern on chart with the CSP in the proper location.

_____   2. Correctly calculated time to complete the search and time to turn for each search leg.

Accomplished   **Mentor signature**_____   **Date**_____

Name: _____

Task COX-06-08-AUX

Task	**Plot A Single-Unit Trackline Return Search Pattern (TSR)**
References	Boat Crew Seamanship Manual, COMDTINST M16114.5 (series), Chapter 15
	U.S. Coast Guard Addendum to the United States National Search and Rescue Supplement (NSS) to the International Aeronautical and Maritime Search and Rescue Manual (IAMSAR), COMDTINST M16130.2 (series), Appendix H
Conditions	Performed at any time ashore. The mentor will provide trainee with a Search Action Plan consisting of: area description (corner point method), pattern designation, number of search legs, Commence Search Point, (CSP), Track Spacing, and search speed.
Standards	Tasks COX-06-05-AUX through COX-06-09-AUX cover the plotting of five search patterns. The trainee will select three and plot **three** of these patterns, based on appropriateness of the patterns for the type of facility and the needs of the operating area.
	In response to the mentor, the trainee will plot a TSR pattern. The pattern must include an estimated time to run. Commence search point must be accurate to within 100 yards, track lines must be within 3 degrees, and times to run within 60 seconds.

Completed	Performance Criteria
_____	1. Correctly laid out search area and pattern on chart with the CSP in the proper location.
_____	2. Correctly calculated time to complete the search..

Accomplished   Mentor signature_____   Date_____

Name: _____

Task COX-06-09-AUX

Task	**Execute A Search Pattern**

References

Boat Crew Seamanship Manual, COMDTINST M16114.5 (series), Chapter 15

U.S. Coast Guard Addendum to the United States National Search and Rescue Supplement (NSS) to the International Aeronautical and Maritime Search and Rescue Manual (IAMSAR), COMDTINST M16130.2 (series), Appendix H

Conditions

Performed underway in calm to moderate weather. The mentor will select a search pattern plotted in Tasks COX-06-05-AUX through COX-06-09-AUX. Use existing wind, current, and weather conditions. The search object is a 14-ft boat.

Standards

The trainee must determine new datum as necessary. The facility shall commence search pattern within 100 yards of CSP. The pattern will be run for a minimum of six legs (SS, PS, or CS) or to completion (VS, TSR or XSB). All turn points must be determined using the most accurate method available to the boat. The search pattern shall be completed within 5 minutes of the calculated completion time.

Completed   **Performance Criteria**

_____   1. Briefed crewmembers on mission.

_____   2. Arrived within 100 yards of plotted CSP.

_____   3. Determined new datum (if necessary).

_____   4. Deployed Datum Marker Bouy (as applicable).

_____   5. Reported on-scene weather to Operational Commander.

_____   6. Ran pattern as previously plotted.

_____   7. Completed turns within 50 yards of plotted positions.

_____   8. Utilized fathometer to verify water depth.

Task COX-06-09-AUX (Continued)

_____   9. Stated SOG.

_____   10. Navigated facility in accordance with Rules of the Road.

_____   11. Identified and utilized aids to navigation.

_____   12. Completed search within 5 minutes of calculated time.

Accomplished   **Mentor signature**_____   **Date**_____

Name: _____

Task COX-06-10-AUX

Task	**Obtain Distress Information And Pass To The Controlling Shore Unit**
References	Boat Crew Seamanship Manual, COMDTINST M16114.5 (series), Chapter 11
Conditions	Performed underway, dock side or ashore. The Mentor will simulate a call from a vessel in distress. The trainee will obtain necessary information from the distressed boat.
Standards	In response to the mentor, the trainee must receive and transmit message traffic using proper radio telephone procedures, including prowords and phonetic alphabet, and identify the voice distress/safety call signals and their frequencies.

Completed   **Performance Criteria**

_____ 1. Identified the voice distress/safety call signals and their broadcast frequency:

   a. MAYDAY, MAYDAY, MAYDAY – Channel 16 (156.8MHZ) or 2182KHZ

   b. PAN PAN, PAN PAN, PAN PAN – Channel 16 or 2182 KHZ

   c. SECURITE, SECURITE, SECURITE – Channel 16 or 2182 KHZ with brief message, then shift to Channel 22A (157.1MHZ) or 2670 KHZ to transmit full message.

_____ 2. Made initial contact with the distressed boat on Channel 16 VHF.

_____ 3. Did not change frequency unless it was necessary.

_____ 4. Requested additional information that may not have been passed during initial MAYDAY transmission:

   a. Name of distressed boat.

   b. Disabled boat's position.

Task COX 06-10-AUX (Continued)

   c. Nature of emergency.

   d. Assistance required.

   e. Number of people on board (POB) and their medical condition.

   f. Boat's description and amount of time boat can stay afloat if sinking.

   g. Emergency equipment onboard.

   h. On scene weather and sea conditions.

_____   5. Transmitted the following radio traffic to the distressed boat broadcasting a MAYDAY:

   a. Name/Number of distressed vessel's name.

   b. "This is Coast Guard Auxiliary Vessel (vessel ID)".

   c. Received MAYDAY.

   d. Allowed short period of time after acknowledging MAYDAY for other stations to acknowledge receipt.

_____   6. Advised distressed boat to have all persons onboard put on life jackets, (PFDs), and to confirm this has been accomplished.

_____   7. Passed your position and estimated time of arrival (ETA) on scene to distressed boat.

_____   8. Kept distressed boat informed of search and rescue effort and set a continuous radio guard.

_____   9. Relayed information to the controlling shore unit as soon as possible.

Accomplished   **Mentor signature**_____   **Date**_____

Section G. Rescue and Assistance

Introduction

The following are the objecives for Section G:

- **Demonstrate** the ability to rescue personnel in various distress situations

- **Demonstrate** the ability to deliver personnel or equipment to vessels in distress

- **Demonstrate** the knowledge and ability to use standard Coast Guard salvage equipment

- **Demonstrate** the knowledge and ability to transfer personnel safely between different types of units

In this section

This section contains four tasks:

Reading Assignments	Task Number	Task	See Page
Ref (b) Chapter 16, Section A Ref (b) Chapter 20,(All)	COX-07-01-AUX	Determine The Approach To An Object And Station Keep	2-68
Ref (b) Chapter 16, Section A	COX-07-02-AUX	Recover A Person From The Water Using The Direct Pick Up Method	2-69
Ref (b) Chapter 18, Section F	COX-07-03-AUX	Approach A Burning Boat And Recover Personnel	2-71
None	COX-07-04-AUX	State The Action To Take If Your Boat Was Aground	2-73

Name: _____

Task COX-07-01-AUX   .

Task	**Determine The Approach To An Object And Station Keep**

References   Boat Crew Seamanship Manual, COMDTINST M16114.5 (series), Chapter 16 and 20

Conditions   Performed underway in calm to moderate conditions. Trainee must accomplish task without prompting or use of a reference.

Standards   In response to the mentor the trainee while operating the boat must determine the approach on a stationary object (buoy, piling, anchored boat, etc) or floating object (boat adrift, life ring, etc.) while using the predominant forces in boat handling. The trainee must then station-keep on the object, at a safe maneuvering distance for the conditions, for 3 minutes in accordance with the steps below.

Completed   **Performance Criteria**

_____   1. Evaluated the water depth and surrounding area for safety of the approach.

_____   2. Positioned the facility at a safe distance and determined the rate of drift between object and facility.

_____   3. Evaluated the predominant forces to determine the approach and station keeping.

_____   4. Briefed the crew of your intentions and their responsibilities.

_____   5. Approached the object at a safe speed.

_____   6. Kept station on the object for 3 minutes.

Accomplished   **Mentor signature**_____   **Date**_____

Name: _____

Task COX-07-02-AUX

Task	**Recover A Person From the Water Using The Direct Pick-Up Method**
References	Boat Crew Seamanship Manual, COMDTINST M16114.5 (series), Chapter 16
Conditions	Performed underway during daylight in calm to moderate seas. Person in the water (PIW) will be simulated with a life-like dummy, fender, or some other floating object. **UNDER NO CIRCUMSTANCES SHOULD A PERSON BE PLACED IN THE WATER.** Trainee must accomplish task without prompting or use of a reference.
Standards	In response to the mentor, after alarm is sounded, the trainee must recover the simulated PIW. The pick-up should be completed within five minutes. **Boat's engine(s) must be in neutral when the PIW is alongside.** The pick-up must be conducted in a manner so as not to endanger the safety of the crew or PIW. Trainee should be able to do the task on the first attempt without extensive maneuvering.

Completed   **Performance Criteria**

_____ 1. After alarm sounded, turned boat in a safe direction.

_____ 2. Assigned crew duties as pointer or recovery pickup man.

_____ 3. Sounded the danger signal (5 or more short blasts).

_____ 4. Marked boat's position by depressing the memory button on the Loran C, or activated the "Man Overboard" function on the GPS, (if available).

_____ 5. Notified controlling authority of Man Overboard and approximate position.

_____ 6. Briefed crew on pick up.

Task COX-07-02-AUX (Continued)

_____ 7. Described the following technics for returning to the PIW.

   a. Stop immediately

   b. Quick turn

   c. Stop and pivot return

   d. Destroyer turn

_____ 8. Determined set and drift for approach based on prevailing weather (predominant forces).

_____ 9. Made approach based on the predominant forces. Facility slowed as final approach made.

_____ 10. Maneuvered alongside PIW.

_____ 11. Placed engine(s) in neutral when PIW was abeam of the boat.

_____ 12. Made all steering adjustments, keeping the boat's stern away from the PIW.

_____ 13. Directed pickup man to recover the PIW at the boat's lowest freeboard.

_____ 14. Ensured crewmembers did not endanger themselves while retrieving PIW.

_____ 15. Made an initial patient assessment and simulated administering first aid as needed.

_____ 16. Notified the controlling authority of PIW's condition.

Accomplished   **Mentor signature**_____   **Date**_____

Name: _____

Task COX-07-03-AUX

Task	**Approach a Burning Boat and Recover Personnel**
References	Boat Crew Seamanship Manual, COMDTINST M16114.5 (series), Chapter 18
Conditions	Performed underway during daylight in fair weather conditions. The distressed boat will simulate having a fire onboard.
Standards	In response to the mentor, the trainee while operating the boat must approach a burning boat (simulated) and recover personnel. Task must be done without endangering either boat or crews.

Completed   **Performance Criteria**

_____   1. Briefed crew and assigned duties (Man Overboard gear, first aid kit, etc. made ready).

_____   2. Established communications with disabled boat and determined:

      a. Number of persons on board

      b. Any persons already in the water

      c. Any injuries or other medical conditions

      d. Instructed persons on board to don life jackets

      e. Passed your intentions to the disabled boat

_____   3. Approached boat from upwind.

_____   4. Rescued all personnel in danger (from the water and/or the boat). Accounted for all personnel from the distressed boat.

_____   5. Made an initial patient assessment and simulated administering first aid as needed.

Task COX-07-03 AUX (Continued)

_____ 6. Informed operational commander or Emergency Medical Service (EMS), as appropriate for situation. Transported personnel as needed.

_____ 7. If no one was injured, set up a safety zone well away from the burning boat. (Asked survivors if there is gasoline, propane or other explosive materials on the boat and where it is located, and passed ht einformation on to the operational commander).

Accomplished Mentor signature_____ Date_____

Name: _____

Task COX-07-04-AUX

Task	**State The Action To Take If Your Boat Was Aground**
References	None
Conditions	Performed at any time ashore, at the dock, or afloat. Trainee must accomplish task without prompting or use of a reference.
Standards	In response to the mentor, the trainee must, without error, state the general action to take if his/her boat was aground.

Completed   **Performance Criteria**

_____   1. Stated that boat's engine(s) should be secured.

_____   2. Stated initial evaluation steps:

        a. Checked personnel for injuries

        b. Ensured boat not taking on water

        c. Notified controlling unit

        d. Took soundings around boat

_____   3. Described the pros and cons of refloating using the following methods:

        a. Backing straight off

        b. Redistribution of weight

        c. Kedging

_____   4. Described the action to take if you can not refloat boat:

        a. Set anchor(s) to prevent boat from being pushed further aground

        b. Set up communications schedule with controlling unit

Accomplished   **Mentor signature**_____   **Date**_____

Section H.   Towing And Salvage

Introduction

The following are the objectives for Section H:

- **Define** and **state** the static and dynamic forces that come into play during various towing evolutions

- **Demonstrate** the procedures used when preparing to take a vessel in tow

- **Demonstrate** the procedures for inspecting both fixed and running towing gear

- **Demonstrate** the procedures for taking a boat in tow using different approaches

In this section

This section contains eight tasks:

Reading Assignments	Task Number	Task	See Page
Ref (b) Chapter 17, (All)	COX-08-01-AUX	State General Towing Safety Precautions	2-75
Ref (b) Chapter 8, Section B Ref (b) Chapter 17, Section B	COX-08-02-AUX	State The Principal Forces That Effect Small Boat Towing	2-76
Ref (b) Chapter 17, Section C	COX-08-03-AUX	Inspect The Towline And Associated Hardware	2-78
Ref (b) Chapter 17, Section D and E	COX-08-04-AUX	Make Preparations For Taking A Vessel In Tow	2-79
Ref (b) Chapter 17, Section D and E	COX-08-05-AUX	Take A Vessel In Stern Tow	2-81
Ref (b) Chapter 17, Section C	COX-08-06-AUX	Use A Shackle Or Kicker/Skiff Hook Assembly Connection To Take A Vessel In Stern Tow	2-83
Ref (b) Chapter 17, Section D	COX-08-07-AUX	Take A Boat In Alongside Tow	2-85
Ref (b) Chapter 17, Section D	COX-08-08-AUX	Moor A Disabled Vessel In Tow To A Float Or Pier	2-87

Name: _____

Task COX-08-01-AUX

Task	**State General Towing Safety Precautions**
References	Boat Crew Seamanship Manual, COMDTINST M16114.5 (series), Chapter 17
Conditions	Performed at any time ashore, at the dock, or afloat. Trainee must accomplish task without prompting or use of a reference.
Standards	In response to the mentor, the trainee must state the general safety towing precautions.

Completed   **Performance Criteria**

_____   1. Stated when to remove personnel from disabled boat.

_____   2. Stated policy on wearing PFDs by personnel aboard the disabled boat.

_____   3. Stated precautions regarding throwing a heaving line.

_____   4. Stated considerations regarding communications establishment and maintenance of a communication schedule with disabled boat.

_____   5. Stated precautions regarding personnel around the towline.

_____   6. Stated precautions regarding the breaking strength and failure of shackles, towlines and bridles.

_____   7. Stated considerations regarding the inspection of deck fittings on the disabled boat.

_____   8. Stated considerations of towing boat's towing capacity and towed boat's capability and hull speed.

Accomplished   **Mentor signature**_____   **Date**_____

Name: _____

Task COX-08-02-AUX

Task	**State The Principal Forces That Effect Small Boat Towing**
References	Boat Crew Seamanship Manual, COMDTINST M16114.5 (series), Chapter 8 and 17
Conditions	Performed at any time ashore, at the dock, or afloat. Trainee must accomplish task without prompting or use of a reference.
Standards	In response to the mentor, the trainee must state the principle forces affecting small boat towing.

Completed   **Performance Criteria**

_____   1. Stated causes and effects of static forces and how to overcome the effect of static force when starting a tow and when changing the towing vessel's heading.

_____   2. Stated types, causes, and effects of dynamic forces.

_____   3. Stated causes of towline strain.

_____   4. Stated cause and effect of shock load and techniques to prevent, counteract, or reduce its effects.

_____   5. Stated effect that the following have on shock load:

   a. Reducing towing speed

   b. Getting the vessels in step

   c. Lengthening the towline

   d. Setting a course to lessen the effect of the seas

   e. Deploying a drogue from the towed vessel

Task COX-08-02-AUX (Continued)

           f. Constantly adjusting the towing vessel's speed to match that of the towed vessel

_____   6. Stated the effect different hull types have on dynamic forces:

           a. Displacement hull

           b. Planing hull

           c. Semi-displacement hull

           d. Multi-hull

Accomplished   **Mentor signature**_____   **Date**_____

Name: _____

Task COX-08-03-AUX

Task	**Inspect The Towline And Associated Hardware**
References	Boat Crew Seamanship Manual, COMDTINST M16114.5 (series), Chapter 17
Conditions	Performed dockside during daylight hours. All lines, bridles, shackles, hooks, and other towing gear carried aboard the facility must be inspected. Trainee must accomplish task without prompting or use of a reference.
Standards	All gear should be inspected in accordance with the above reference and as outlined in the steps below.

Completed	Performance Criteria
_____	1. Towline inspected, warning signs of wear or defective condition stated.
_____	2. Bridles inspected, warning signs of wear or defective condition stated.
_____	3. Shackles and kicker/skiff hook inspected, warning signs of wear or defective condition stated.
_____	4. Bitts, cleats, chocks, and other associated towing gear inspected, warning signs of wear or defective condition stated.

Accomplished   Mentor signature_____   Date_____

Name: _____

Task COX-08-04-AUX

Task	**Make Preparations For Taking A Vessel In Tow**
References	Boat Crew Seamanship Manual, COMDTINST M16114.5 (series), Chapter 17
Conditions	Performed at any time underway in calm conditions. Trainee must accomplish task without prompting or use of a reference.
Standards	In response to the mentor, the trainee must make necessary preparations to take a vessel in tow in accordance with the steps outlined below.

Completed   **Performance Criteria**

_____   1. Communications established with vessel to be towed.

_____   2. Performed an on-scene assessment of the disabled vessel's material condition.

_____   3. Determined physical condition of the people on board the disabled vessel.

_____   4. Directed people on board disabled vessel to don life jackets.

_____   5. Determined the rate of drift and approach to make.

_____   6. Briefed crew and assigned duties.

_____   7. Briefed disabled vessels crew on:

        a.   Transfer of crew or equipment prior to towing

        b.   Hookup procedure

        c.   Line handling

        d.   Emergency breakaway communications/signals

Task COX-08-04-AUX (Continued)

e. General safety during the approach, passing of towline and the towing evolution

f. Chafing gear fitting for towing line or bridle

g. Operating procedure (steering behind, etc.)

h. Towing approach

_____ 8. Towline rigged for passing to the disabled vessel.

_____ 9. Communications schedule established with disabled vessel, for the duration of the tow.

_____ 10. Ensured that the operator of the disabled vessel understands the above procedures.

Accomplished **Mentor signature**_____ **Date**_____

Name: _____

Task COX-08-05-AUX

Task	**Take A Vessel In Stern Tow**
References	Boat Crew Seamanship Manual, COMDTINST M16114.5 (series), Chapter 17
Conditions	Performed underway in calm to moderate weather conditions. Two boats are required. The towed vessel must be within the towing vessel's maximum towing capabilities.
Standards	In response to the mentor, the trainee must take a vessel in stern tow. The trainee must be at the helm and operating the facility. A heaving line must be used to pass the towline. A bridle may be used for hooking up. Task must be done without endangering boats or crews.

Completed   **Performance Criteria**

_____ 1. Made preparations for taking a boat in stern tow in accordance with Task COX-08-04-AUX.

_____ 2. Maneuvered boat onto the same heading as the disabled vessel and stopped astern of it.

_____ 3. Determined vessels relative rate of drift by observing which vessel drifts to leeward faster.

_____ 4. Made approach into predominate weather/seas.

_____ 5. Performed station keeping in optimal position.

_____ 6. Towline passed using heaving line, if necessary.

_____ 7. Line paid out and tended away from screws.

_____ 8. A working turn placed on tow bitt or cleat(s) after towline is secured on disabled vessel.

Task COX-00-05-AUX (Continued)

_____ 9. Initial course set and directed crew to pay out appropriate length of towline for the size and type of boat being towed.

_____ 10. Made up tow bitt.

_____ 11. Adjusted scope of towline to put towed vessel in step.

_____ 12. Towing watch set and maintained.

_____ 13. Installed chafing gear as needed.

_____ 14. Maintained safe towing speed.

_____ 15. Checked status of towed vessel.

Accomplished   **Mentor signature**_____ **Date**_____

Name: _____

Task COX-08-06-AUX

Task	**Use A Shackle Or Kicker/Skiff Hook Assembly Connection To Take A Vessel In Stern Tow**
References	Boat Crew Seamanship Manual, COMDTINST M16114.5 (series), Chapter 17
Conditions	Performed underway in calm weather conditions. Two boats are required. The towed vessel must be within the towing vessel's maximum towing capabilities.
Standards	In response to the mentor, the trainee must use a kicker/skiff hook to take a vessel in stern tow. Task must be done without endangering either boat or crew.

Completed   **Performance Criteria**

_____ 1. Made preparations for taking a boat in tow in accordance with Task COX-08-04-AUX.

_____ 2. Began approach from off the bow and down wind of the disabled vessel.

_____ 3. Maneuvered boat to position in front of the disabled vessel.

_____ 4. Performed station keeping in optimal position, close enough to pass the shackle or attach the skiff hook.

_____ 5. Directed crewmember to attach shackle or pass the skiff hook to the disabled boat.

_____ 6. Paid out and tended line away from screws.

_____ 7. Placed working turn on tow bitt or cleat(s) after towline is secured on disabled vessel.

_____ 8. Set initial course.

_____ 9. Directed crew to pay out appropriate length of towline.

Task COX-08-0C-AUX (Continued)

_____ 10. Towing watch set and maintained.

_____ 11. Adjusted scope of towline to put boats in step.

_____ 12. Chafing gear installed (if needed).

_____ 13. Maintained safe towing speed.

_____ 14. Checked status of towed vessel.

_____ 15. Moor a disabled vessel from a side tow.

Accomplished   Mentor signature_____ **Date**_____

Name: _____

Task COX-08-07-AUX

Task	**Take A Boat In Alongside Tow**
References	Boat Crew Seamanship Manual, COMDTINST M16114.5 (series), Chapter 17
Conditions	Performed underway in calm weather. Two boats are needed. The towed vessel must be within the towing vessel's maximum towing capabilities. Trainee must accomplish task without prompting or use of a reference.
Standards	In response to the mentor, the trainee must transition from stern tow to alongside tow. All line handling commands must be given and received in a loud/clear voice using proper commands. Task must be done without endangering either boat or crew.

Completed   **Performance Criteria**

_____   1. Briefed crew and assigned duties. Emphasized the necessity for
                 communications between crew and coxswain.

_____   2. Briefed operator of the towed boat on procedure to be used.

_____   3. Prepared deck for alongside tow.

                 a. Rigged fenders on appropriate side of tow vessel.

                 b. Made alongside lines ready.

_____   4. Slowed speed in increments and shortened tow if needed. Maintained
                 positive control of the tow, kept towline in view and appropriate relative
                 position while shortening tow.

_____   5. Broke down tow bitt (if equipped), hauled slack towline aboard and faked out
                 of the way.

_____   6. Dropped towline of disabled vessel (for free approach), or properly executed
                 a backdown approach.

Task COX-08-07-AUX (Continued)

_____ 7. Moved towline to the #1 line position (bowline) or replaced towline with another line.

_____ 8. Secured the bowline (#1 line) to forward cleat/bitt.

_____ 9. Passed and secured tow strap (#2 line) to disabled boat ensuring the stern of the boat is aft of the towed boat.

_____ 10. Directed crew to pass and establish control of stern line (#4 line).

_____ 11. Directed crew to pass and establish control of backing line (#3 line).

_____ 12. Passed eye of all lines to towed boat and working ends used on the facility.

_____ 13. Tow strap tightened by facility going astern, pulling in slack, and securing the line.

_____ 14. All other lines adjusted by vessel gaining headway, taking up slack, and lines secured.

NOTE: The stern tow can be shifted to an alongside tow by walking the towline forward and using it as the #1 line (bow line). Or the towline may be disconnected after slowing the tow, and a free approach to the disabled boat can be made to take the boat alongside.

Accomplished   Mentor signature_____   Date_____

Name: _____

Task COX-08-08-AUX

Task | **Moor A Disabled Vessel In Tow To A Float Or Pier**

References — Boat Crew Seamanship Manual, COMDTINST M16114.5 (series), Chapter 17

Conditions — Performed at any time ashore, at the dock, or afloat. Trainee must accomplish task without prompting or use of a reference. Performed underway in calm seas. Two boats are required.

Standards — In response to the mentor, the trainee must moor a disabled vessel in tow to a float or pier. Trainee must be at the helm and operating the facility. Task must be done without endangering personnel or boat. Towline must not be placed near the screws at any time.

Completed   **Performance Criteria**

_____ 1. Stated the expected effects of the wind and current on the mooring of the boat.

_____ 2. Briefed crew on the procedure to be used and their duties. Emphasized the necessity for communications between crew and coxswain.

_____ 3. Briefed operator of the towed boat on mooring method and location.

_____ 4. Briefed bow pointer and positioned in effective location.

_____ 5. Approached dock slowly at an angle.

_____ 6. Directed crewmember standing on bow to give distances to the pier or float.

_____ 7. Moored disabled boat (or larger of two boats) against pier or float.

_____ 8. Directed crewmember on bow to secure bowline (#1 line) or after bow spring line, (#2 line).

_____ 9. Pivoted stern of towed boat (or larger boat) towards dock.

_____ 10. Directed crew to secure stern line, then the two side mooring lines.

Accomplished   **Mentor signature**_____ **Date**_____

Section I. Auxiliary Specific Tasks

Introduction

The following are the objectives for Section I:

- **Demonstrate** the ability to perform various Auxiliary administrative and "command" duties.

- **Demonstrate** competency to perform as an Auxiliary Coxswain on an operational facility.

In this section

This section contains six tasks:

Reading Assignments	Task Number	Task	See Page
Ref (b) Chapter 2, Section B	COX-09-01-AUX	Discuss Auxiliary Patrol Commander's Duties **(Waiverable by DIRAUX)**	2-89
Ref (d) Chapter 2, Section A Ref (d) Chapter 4, Section A	COX-09-02-AUX	Complete Administrative Tasks (Reports, Orders, Etc.)	2-91
Ref (d) Chapters 1-5 Ref (f) Chapter 4	COX-09-03-AUX	Complete The Operations Policy Manual And National SAR Plan Open Book Exam	2-92
Ref (b) Chapter 1, Section C Ref (b) Chapter 14, (All)	COX-09-04-AUX	Perform A Night Navigation And Piloting Exercise **(Waiverable by DIRAUX)**	2-93
None	COX-09-05-AUX	Dockside Oral Exam	2-95
None	COX-09-06-AUX	Underway Check Ride	2-97

Name: _____

Task COX-09-01-AUX

Task	**Discuss Auxiliary Patrol Commander's Duties (Waiverable By DIRAUX)**
References	Boat Crew Seamanship Manual, COMDTINST M16114.5 (series), Chapter 2
Conditions	Performed ashore. The mentor will provide the trainee with information and requirements about a simulated marine parade or regatta.
Standards	In response to the mentor, the trainee must discuss the duties and responsibilities of an Auxiliary Patrol Commander (AUXPATCOM) for a marine event. **NOTE:** May be waived by the Director in accordance with Section 1.B.4.

<u>**Completed**</u>   <u>**Performance Criteria**</u>

_____ 1. Obtained a copy of the approved application(s), written instructions, or authority for event.

_____ 2. Obtained and studied any specific additional instructions.

_____ 3. Coordinated with sponsor and law enforcement agencies.

_____ 4. Established fixed and/or moving sectors using given information (course, route, etc.).

_____ 5. Determined patrol requirements (boats, radio facilities, crews, etc.).

_____ 6. Ensured arrangements made for the proper facilities to be available.

_____ 7. Briefed all parties on their duties and responsibilities; ensured all boats are in proper trim (flags, signs, neat appearance, etc.) and crews in proper uniform.

_____ 8. Selected a AUXPATCOM vantage point with visibility and mobility in mind.

_____ 9. Established communication frequencies and network.

Task COX-09-01 AUX (Continued)

_____ 10. Deployed facilities to their patrol positions.

_____ 11. Ensured all debris and spectator boats are clear of the patrol area.

_____ 12. Monitored and ensured receipt of all casualty reports.

_____ 13. Dispatched a facility to assist as needed or stop event if necessary.

_____ 14. Ensured area cleared after completion of the event.

_____ 15. Completed required after action reports.

Accomplished   **Mentor signature**_____   **Date**_____

Name: _____

Task COX-09-02-AUX

Task | **Complete Administrative Tasks (Reports, Orders, Etc.)**

References | Auxiliary Operations Policy Manual, COMDTINST M16798.3 (series), Chapters 2 and 4

Various Forms Instructions

District Director's procedures for submitting forms

Conditions | Performed at any time ashore, at the dock, or afloat. Trainee may use instructions for filling out the forms, and must follow the most current district/area procedures for submitting forms.

Standards | In response to the mentor, the trainee must demonstrate the ability to prepare and submit forms associated with Auxiliary patrols under Coast Guard orders, and the procedures to follow if involved in a mishap.

Completed | **Performance Criteria**

_____ 1. Prepared Activity Report-Mission, ANSC 7030.

_____ 2. Prepared ANSC-7034/CG-4612, Auxiliary SAR Incident Report.

_____ 3. Obtained partol orders from the Patrol Orders Management System (POMS) and completed a CG-5132, Coast Guard Auxiliary Patrol Order.

_____ 4. Stated reference sources to follow if involved in a boat mishap.

_____ 5. Described distribution of the above forms and submission requirements.

Accomplished | **Mentor signature**_____ **Date**_____

Name: _____

Task COX-09-03-AUX

Task	**Complete the Operations Policy Manual and National SAR Plan Open Book Exam**
References	Auxiliary Operations Policy Manual, COMDTINST M16798.3 (series), Chapters 1 thru 5
	U.S. Coast Guard Addendum to the United States National Search and Rescue Supplement (NSS) to the International Aeronautical and Maritime Search and Rescue Manual (IAMSAR), COMDTINST M16130.2 (series), Chapter 4
Conditions	Task is conducted at the dock or online. Trainee may accomplish task with the use of a reference.
Standards	The Trainee must have a score of 90% or better.

<u>**Completed**</u>   <u>**Performance Criteria**</u>

_____   1.   Passed the open book Operations Policy Manual and National SAR Plan exam.

Accomplished   **Mentor signature**_____   **Date**_____

Name: _____

Task COX-09-04-AUX

Task	**Perform a Night Navigation and Piloting Exercise (Waiverable by DIRAUX)**
References	Boat Crew Seamanship Manual, COMDTINST M16114.5 (series), Chapter 14
Conditions	Performed at the dock and underway in calm conditions on a clear night. The trainee must use crewmembers and available equipment to integrate information and safely navigate the facility. All chart work, including courses, distances, time to run and electronics set up shall be completed prior to getting underway. Trainee must accomplish task without prompting or use of a reference.
Standards	In response to the mentor, the trainee must perform a nighttime navigation and piloting exercise. After receiving position (given by the mentor), the trainee should plot a course, determine an ETA, and get the facility underway within 30 minutes of notification.
	NOTE: May be waived by the Director in accordance with Section 1.B.4. If waived, candidate must discuss night navigation and piloting.

Completed   **Performance Criteria**

_____   1. Compass course laid out on the chart indicating predicted turns, and ETA established

_____   2. Conducted a pre-underway check off and confirmed the facility was within its stated operational limitations to perform the assigned mission.

_____   3. Conducted a pre-underway brief.

_____   4. Ensured all crewmembers wore PFDs and had a good understanding of the use of the personnel survival equipment. Tested electronic Personal Marker Lights (PMLs).

_____   5. Departed within 30 minutes of notification.

_____   6. Efficiently and safely handled the facility and communicated effectively with crewmembers while getting underway.

Task COX-09-04-AUX (Continued)

_____ 7. Piloted by dead reckoning and/or "Seaman's Eye". Considered and adjusted for the effects of:

     a. Tide

     b. Currents

     c. Wind and weather conditions

     d. Navigational hazards

_____ 8. Used manual and electronic navigational equipment to determine position and adjust DR and ETA for safe navigation.

_____ 9. Properly assigned and utilized crewmembers.

_____ 10. Arrived within 10 minutes of ETA and 500 yards of given position.

Note: Although the 10 minute ETA is desirable it should not over ride safety or other factors which would hinder safe navigation.

_____ 11. Effectively used risk management and team coordination with crewmembers.

Accomplished **Mentor signature**_____ **Date**_____

Name: _____

Task COX-09-05-AUX

Task

Dockside Oral And Written Examination

References

Boat Crew Seamanship Manual, COMDTINST M16114.5 (series)

Auxiliary Operations Policy Manual, COMDTINST M16798.3 (series)

District Standard Operating Procedures, Policy Manuals, and other local Instructions

Conditions

Performed ashore or aboard a moored facility.

Standards

The trainee must successfully demonstrate knowledge of qualification tasks selected by the QE. The QE will select at least one task from each section (A – I) of the Qualification Guide, plus one task of the QE's choice, as outlined by the performance criteria below. The QE may ask questions based on additional tasks as required to ensure that the trainee is fully ready to be qualified.

Completed   **Performance Criteria**

_____   1. Section A, COX-01-_____-AUX

_____   2. Section B, COX-02-_____-AUX

_____   3. Section C, COX-03-_____-AUX

_____   4. Section D, COX-04-_____-AUX

_____   5. Section E, COX-05-_____-AUX

_____   6. Section F, COX-06-_____-AUX

_____   7. Section G, COX-07-_____-AUX

_____   8. Section H, COX-08-_____-AUX

Task COX-00-05-AUX (Continued)

_____ 9. Section I, COX-09-____-AUX

_____ 10. COX-____-____-AUX

Accomplished

QE's signature_____ **Date**_____

QE's signature_____ **Date**_____

Comments

Name: _____

Task COX-09-06-AUX

Task	**Underway Check Ride**

References	Boat Crew Seamanship Manual, COMDTINST M16114.5 (series)
	Auxiliary Operations Policy Manual, COMDTINST M16798.3 (series)
	District Standard Operating Procedures, Policy Manuals, and other local Instructions

Conditions	Performed underway on an Auxiliary Facility in calm sea conditions. Trainee must accomplish task without prompting or use of a reference. COX-01-01-AUX through COX-09-04-AUX **must** be satisfactorily completed prior to conducting this underway check ride.

Standards	In response to the QE and being overseen by the Coxswain, the trainee must answer questions on, and perform the below listed evolutions, for the Coxswain position.
	NOTE: The QE may add tasks to the performance criteria if he/she feels it necessary to evaluate a trainee's readiness for qualification. The addition of any tasks will be reported to Commandant (CG-3PCX-2) via the Director of Auxiliary for possible inclusion in future revisions of the program.

Completed	**Performance Criteria**
_____	1. Conducted a pre-underway check off and confirmed the facility was within its stated operational limitations to perform the assigned mission.
_____	2. Conducted a pre-underway brief. Assessed crewmembers physical capabilities to perform mission, discussed safety issues, such as:
	a. Wearing of jewelry
	b. Team coordination and communication
	c. Operational Risk Management
_____	3. Ensured all crewmembers wore PFDs and had a good understanding of the requirements and use of the personnel survival equipment.
_____	4. Efficiently and safely handled the facility and communicated effectively with the crew while getting underway.

Task COX-09-06-AUX (Continued)

_____ 5. Gave proper commands to the helm watch, used navigational charts, aids to navigation, and installed electronic navigation gear.

_____ 6. Assigned lookout watch(es) and verified the safety of the facility based on the reports made by lookout.

_____ 7. Responded to a Man-Overboard drill, and safely recovered a simulated PIW. (A life ring, life-like dummy, or other floating object can be used as PIW).

_____ 8. Demonstrated proficiency and safety during a stern tow, including:

   a. Making preparations for taking a vessel in tow.

   b. Communication with crewmembers.

   c. Towing approach and station keeping.

   d. Proper speed and towline considered.

   e. Safety of and communications with personnel on towed boat.

_____ 9. Demonstrated proficiency and safety during an alongside tow.

_____ 10. Safely moored a disabled vessel in tow to a float or a pier.

_____ 11. Correctly plotted and ran three legs of a search pattern designated by the QE.

_____ 12. Demonstrated proficiency while anchoring and weighing anchor.

_____ 13. Used appropriate navigational sound signals when needed.

_____ 14. Correctly piloted and labeled navigational charts during a three leg course run given by the QE. Some or all of the following were demonstrated, as needed, during the run:

   a. Correctly converted from true to compass course.

   b. Speed, Time, and Distance computed.

   c. ETA computed within a reasonable time.

   d. Set and Drift calculated to correct course and speed.

   e. Fixes taken and properly labeled to verify facility's position.

_____ 15. Kept the controlling unit informed of mission operations and conducted scheduled Position and Ops Normal Reports.

Task COX-09-06-AUX (Continued)

_____ 16. Efficiently and safely moored the boat.

_____ 17. Satisfactorily answered QEs questions on policies and procedures. Questions are limited to knowledge required by the qualification guide tasks, (e.g. engine casualties, SAR organization and responsibilities, MSAP, salvage policy, patrol commander's duties).

_____ 18. Discussed and demonstrated knowledge of filling out and processing required reports.

Accomplished QE's signature_____ Date_____

QE's signature_____ Date_____

Comments **NOTE-** Comments should be made in detail. Tasks that were not performed to standards require specific comments addressing what the deficiencies were and why, and what corrective action must be taken to be successful at the next check ride. Each QE should initial on the line by the task that was successfully accomplished during the check ride they evaluated and then sign on the "Accomplished" and "Date" line. A copy of this task sheet should accompany the letter for Recommend for Certification, to the Operations Training Officer.

(Additional comments may be recorded on a separate sheet and attached to the checklist)